A MISSING CHAPTER
OF THE
INDIAN MUTINY

A MISSING CHAPTER
OF THE
INDIAN MUTINY

CHARLES LIONEL SHOWERS

GYAN

Published by

Gyan Publishing House
5, Ansari Road
Daryaganj, New Delhi-110002
Phone: 011-47034999, 9811692060
E-mail: books@gyanbooks.com

Distribution Network
gyanbooks.com
India, USA, Canada, UK, Australia

ISBN: 978-93-6920-416-8 (PB)

First Published, 1888

2nd Impression 2025

Printed at: Gyan Press, Delhi.

A MISSING CHAPTER OF THE INDIAN MUTINY
Author: CHARLES LIONEL SHOWERS

A MISSING CHAPTER OF THE INDIAN MUTINY.

AN INTERIOR VIEW IN CHITORE,

WITH THE COLUMN OF VICTORY.

A MISSING CHAPTER

OF THE

INDIAN MUTINY.

BY

LIEUT.-GENERAL CHARLES LIONEL SHOWERS,

Political Resident in the Meywar States (Rajpûtâna), during the period in question.

London:

LONGMANS, GREEN AND CO.

AND NEW YORK: 15, EAST 16TH STREET.

1888.

PREFACE.

THE events related in the following pages will not be found recorded in the Blue Book of the Indian Mutiny—my official reports, as Political Resident at the Meywar States during the period in question, not having been included in that document presented to Parliament in obedience to its order. Having recently, in clearing out a long disused cabinet, lit upon copies of the reports in question, together with a mass of correspondence, including some letters in original from Lieut.-Colonel, afterwards General Sir George Lawrence, my immediate predecessor in the Meywar Residency, I find myself in a position to supplement the history of the period with respect to events within the Meywar States as yet untold. These documents may afford some clue further to the miscarriage of my reports in transmission through the office of the Agent Governor-General, Colonel Lawrence, who, at the period in question, had been promoted to the superior office on the transfer to Lucknow at that juncture of his brother Sir Henry Lawrence. I forbear, however, to obtrude them on the reader at the opening of my narrative, and thus detain him from the perusal of stirring events and incidental episodes which I venture to hope may prove not without interest. The documents in question, then, I refer to in a Supplementary Chapter, appending vouchers, and will ask the reader to turn to it before closing the book for matter of exposition as well as of general interest. Few incidents of the period could exceed in pathos the late Sir Henry Lawrence's dying appeal to the Maharana of Oodeypore, which closes the chapter.

In proceeding now to recount the events of the troubled period of the Mutiny as experienced within the circle of my extensive official charge, I purpose quoting generally from my unpublished Reports and Diaries and Correspondence of the period, in order that the incidents may be presented in succession to the reader with the greater fidelity and graphic force as life-photographs taken at the time.

The historic land-marks left by the events about to be related in this missing chapter of the Indian Mutiny, may serve to complete the history of its suppression by such a numerically inferior and scattered force of the English race, as seemed, at the time, almost to preclude hope. In depositing that record of achievement, then, upon the shelves of the National archives, the people of England would not, I believe, willingly see it curtailed by one line of recorded honest effort.

Some of the most important of the questions discussed in the series of brilliant articles on "The India of the Queen," which have recently appeared in the columns of the *Times*, will be found raised by the events narrated in the following pages, and by the incidents of the Mutiny generally. On some of these questions the views of the correspondent of the *Times* will find here corroborative illustration; whilst in regard to others, instances in opposition to the conclusions arrived at by him will claim recognition. The arguments on either side will be set forth in a concluding review to enable the reader to form a judgment on the momentous question propounded in the concluding article of the series—"WHITHER?"

C. L. SHOWERS.

LYMINGTON,
HANTS.
January, 1888.

CONTENTS.

APPENDIX.

ILLUSTRATIONS.

THE MEYWAR STATES OF RAJPUTANA IN THE INDIAN MUTINY.

CHAPTER I.

STORM SIGNALS: CONE HOISTED TO THE EAST.

TO an observer in India who had been watching the incipient indications at once of discontent in the Native Army, and of secret collusion or combination on the part of the country at large—partial mutinies and nightly incendiarisms on the one side, the circulation of secret signs, posting of threatening placards, &c., on the other—and who traced those alarming symptoms to causes long in operation, to such the outburst of military revolt and organized rebellion at Meerut and Delhie, on the 10th and 11th May, 1857, came in no wise as an unlooked-for sequel to the premonitory portents. To such an observer, then, the personal incidents of this first crash, unparalleled in their ruthless barbarity, had significance chiefly as proclaiming that a struggle for Empire had begun—that India was in danger,—and that all possible effort on the part of every officer at his post, of every Englishman in his place, and the most consummate forethought in the application of our reliable resources would be needed to save the country.

My own official action during the crisis being taken upon my view of the vast significance of the opening events here adverted to, a reference to one or two circumstances in proof of my right apprehension of the same may serve to explain that action at critical conjunctures.

Recurring first to the memorandum, on the Annexation policy, which I had had the honour of placing on record at the Board of Control, India Office, in the preceding Spring, 1856, I brought out a copy of the document when returning to India in the autumn of that year, and submitted it to the Governor-General Lord Canning's perusal, through his private secretary, the Hon. Gerald Talbot. His Lordship kept the paper for over a month, and frequently in conversation recurred, Mr. Talbot mentioned to me from time to time, to my arguments against the policy in question. "Captain Showers' views," the Governor-General would observe, "seem most conclusive; but what he advocates would involve a reversal of the policy which I am sent to carry out, viz., the consolidation of the Empire through the absorption of the Native States."

No change, however, was made in the policy in question, to reassure the princes against the contemplated subversion of their dynasties by the prohibition, in contravention of the immemorial usage of the country, to adopt heirs in failure of lineal descendants. That policy was inaugurated by the annexation of Satara, a measure taken in direct opposition to the views regarding the succession placed on record by Sir George Clerk, in his official position as Governor of Bombay. In his minute dated 12th April, 1848, reviewing the whole question raised by the death of the late Rajah without lineal descendant, he based his views on the terms of the Treaty of 1819, concluded with the Satara State. Therein the succession of the State in perpetuity, guaranteed to the then reigning Rajah's "heirs and successors," Sir George contended, must be interpreted according to the immemorial usage of the country, and that the lad adopted by the late Rajah was such a successor. He added, "whatever we intend in favour of an ally in perpetuity, when executing a treaty with him on that basis, by that we ought to abide in our relations with his successor.

In the present instance the terms and intentions of the Treaty appear to me to be remarkably distinct and perspicuous. Should any doubt be entertained, Mr. Elphinstone and Captain Grant Duff, under whose direction it was drawn, could be referred to as to their understanding of the words at the time the treaty was concluded." Such high-minded and just principles of action must have commanded assent on the part of the Supreme and Home Government, apart from the high authority on which the proposed measure based on them was supported, had not the annexation been a foregone conclusion. Lord Dalhousie's views in regard to his anticipated consolidation of the Indian empire by the absorption of the Native States, were passed fully under review by the Home Government, and carried by an overwhelming majority of the Court of Directors. Four able dissentients, who placed on record their minutes of dissent, were overruled. From that day State after State fell in on failure of lineal descendants until the last—Oude—which was annexed by the deposition of the King on moral grounds.

Lord Canning, accordingly, having received his mandate, considered that he had no option. The conspirators of the revolutionary movement, not being counteracted by any practical exhibition on the part of Government of a conservative tendency, were left to work out their ends by the masterly stroke of combining both sections of the Native Army—Mahomedan and Hindoo—in an apprehension for the integrity of their respective religions, by the instigation that the Government designed to absorb both in a general Christian propagandism. The fiction of the greased cartridge for the new rifle being prepared with pig's fat and bullock's fat, was implicitly believed by the uneducated rank and file of the army, and thus by a master-stroke both of the hereditarily antagonistic sections were combined in one common crusade against the supposed perfidious subverters of both religions.

While waiting however for an expected signal for a simultaneous rise, the troops generally dissembled well, remaining steady to routine duty and respectful to their officers, so that it was believed, and by none more hopefully than the Government, that the restiveness exhibited here and there was but a passing ebullition of partial discontent from possibly local or personal causes. At this juncture, I wrote in April my views regarding the situation to the Political Resident of Bhopal, eliciting the following reply: "I hope your dreary anticipations of coming evils to India will not be realized. I do not think there is much danger in the direction you point at—among the Native Army." Within less than a month from that date the crash came—prematurely precipitated by the imprisonment of the 3rd Cavalry men at Meerut. And it must be considered fortunate for us that it was so precipitated. Otherwise, in the fulness of time, the machinations of the astute conspirators would have been fully effected by the simultaneous rise of the rebels at all points on the preconcerted signal and watchword: *"A star shall fall!"* From the overwhelming catastrophe that such an event must have occasioned, we were saved by but an accident.

How little of right apprehension of the situation there was on the part of Lord Canning's official advisers, may be gathered from the Government despatch cited by the *Westminster*, in an article of 1865, reviewing Kaye's "Sepoy War," and from which I quote the following passage :—

"How little of right apprehension there was in the council of the Governor-General of India, of the dark shadows thrown before by the coming events, may be gathered from the despatch of the Government of India to the Court of Directors, dated May 19th, 1857, reporting the Mutiny, and written in full knowledge of the rise of the Native troops at Meerut and Delhi, of the ruthless massacres which had attended the revolt, and crowned by the seizure of the ancient Imperial Capital, and proclamation of the restored Mogul dynasty. What was the view taken by the Government of those events, and the remedial measure which it submitted for the approval of the Home Government? Let us hear the despatch. After enumerating by numbers the six regiments which had been concerned in the rise at Meerut and Delhi, the despatch observes: 'Thus, at the present moment the Native strength of the Bengal estabiishment is reduced by six regiments. We recommend that the six Native regiments which are in effect no longer in existence, should not be replaced, whereby the establishment of the regiments of Native Infantry would be reduced to sixty-eight regiments, and that the European officers of these late regiments should be used to officer three regiments of Europeans, to be added to your establishment at this Presidency.' As if the defection of the six mutinied regiments were the first and last of the terrible drama upon which the curtain had but just risen in yells and flames of successful revolt, in shrieks of slaughtered women, and in the pealing proclamation of a restored dynasty!"

CHAPTER II.

OUTBURST OF THE MUTINY.

THE first intelligence of the outburst reached me on the 18th May at Mount Aboo, where I had been summoned for an official conference by Colonel Lawrence. The proceedings of this Conference were naturally intensified by the exigencies of the crisis and protracted from day to day till all necessary measures had been taken. Foremost among these I wrote to my friend, the late lamented Lieut.-General Ashburnham, who was expected to touch at Bombay *en route* to China as Commander-in-Chief of the force despatched from England for the China war. In communicating the intelligence of the rising at Meerut and Delhie, I submitted to his judgment, matured by long experience with Indian affairs, to weigh the character of the emergency that had arisen, when, should it appear to him as to myself that India was in danger, I ventured to express my assurance that he would not hesitate to arrange for his China battalions being intercepted at Singapore, and diverted to Calcutta to meet the paramount call for reinforcements that had arisen in India. On the breaking up of the Conference at

Aboo I returned to my own post of Oodeypore, riding by double marches across the range of Aravulli Mountains running between Aboo and that capital, arriving on the 29th idem (May). At the close of the last day's journey I had proposed to ride straight into the capital, waiving the usual ceremony of Peshwai, or State reception, as my entry might be thrown late in the night. But the Maharana sent out a confidential officer to meet me and overrule my proposed plan on account of the disturbances that had broken out, it occurring to His Highness with thoughtful consideration that my entering the capital without the usual State Peshwai, might, at so critical a conjuncture, be construed by the ill-disposed into an intentional slight, and thus possibly endanger my safety. By his express desire, then, and through the hospitality of its lord, Rao Bukht Singh, the Rao of Bedla, I stopped overnight at that castle and made my public entry the following morning in the usual form, the Maharana coming out to Peshwai to the Choghan, or Champs de Mars, in more than usual state to receive me.

This was but the beginning of the Maharana's thoughtful care for the personal safety of the British Representative at his Court. Being absolutely alone at the time at Oodeypore without my escort, or even my office establishment, and the capital being filled with fanatic mercenary troops, Mahomedan and other, similar to those at the hands of whom my brother Political Agents on either side of my post, Major Burton in Harrowtee and Captain Monck Mason in Marwar, subsequently lost their lives, the Maharana proposed that I should take up my residence in the Water Palace of one of the islands of the lake; but I declined to do so, as any step on the part of the British Representative indicative of a want of confidence in our position, was specially to be avoided at such a time. The Residency, then, being wholly without defences, his Highness sent for my protection four of the chiefs who were in personal attendance on himself at the palace. These, with their respective retainers, kept watch and ward day and night.

Intelligence of the events at Meerut and Delhie had already reached Oodeypore. Public excitement was great, and was increased by the news, which reached the Capital a day or two after my arrival, of the rising of the troops at Nusseerabad on the 28th. The mutiny among the Bengal troops, manifestly spreading, was already in the heart of Rajputana. Then first arose rumours of an approaching rise at Neemuch, the principal military post within my political circle, distant eighty miles from the Capital, where was stationed the strongest Native Brigade of troops in India, horse, foot and guns, unchecked by the presence of a single European soldier of the line. These rumours served to intensify the excitement at Oodeypore, where were quartered some of the Durbar's regiments of regulars

(Pultuns) composed principally of the same classes of mixed Hindoos and Mussulmen as filled our own Native Army ranks. I was hooted in passing through the city to visit the Maharana in his palace. Expresses, which I forwarded on regularly to the Officiating Agent Governor-General, and to the Foreign Secretary, brought me, at all hours of the day and night, from Colonel Abbott, commanding at Neemuch, and Captain Lloyd, Superintendent of the Jawad Neemuch District, varying accounts of the temper of the troops. Now, that they were on the brink of revolt: again, that the crisis had passed over, and confidence reviving. At one moment urging me to march with the Raj troops on Neemuch; at the next, begging me on no account to bring a Raj soldier within sight of the Cantonment.

In view of so conflicting a state of matters at Neemuch, I thought the best thing I could do was to ride straight in, alone, and move up some of the Rana's troops to the contiguous frontier post of Chota Sadree, so as to be within call. I wrote to Colonel Abbott of my intention, and suggested his sending out an escort of his Regular Cavalry to meet me, if he thought such exhibition of confidence in his men would tend to keep them steady.

My preparations were made. The time (on the 3rd June) of my intended departure from Oodeypore was at hand, when a hurried unfinished express from Lloyd, dated 11 a.m. of the preceding day, was received, announcing the state of matters at

Neemuch as nearly desperate, that the troops had obtained *on demand* ammunition for the guns, and were on the point of rising.

My contemplated journey alone was thus arrested. It only remained to move on Neemuch with Raj troops.

But how to get them? The Maharana seemed stunned with the fast-following blows to our power which threatened to leave him to combat alone the serious combination of disaffected Meywar Chiefs which had been banded against his authority in a smouldering chronic rebellion for some years previously. Nothing was talked of among the Ministers but concentrating the Durbar forces at Oodeypore.

This policy would most probably have been fatal to our position in Meywar, and certainly, as it turned out, to the British refugees who fled westward on the revolt of the Neemuch brigade (on the 3rd).

Impressed with the vital importance of open and active co-operation on the part of the Maharana, I sought an interview with His Highness.

Aware that in the excited state of feeling among his foreign mercenaries, my recent passage through the city to Durbar had nearly precipitated an *émeute*, His Highness in acceding to my request proposed that we should meet on the margin of the lake, indicating a spot as the rendezvous to which he would cross in boats.

At the interview thus considerately arranged, seated together on a carpet spread on the bank, all attendants being retired out of ear-shot, the subject of the Mutiny was discussed in all its bearings. The most important question was, how far the revolt would spread. Having long foreseen and placed on record my view of the danger of a general rising of the Native Army, I did not disguise my opinion that the Mutiny would be general, and that our position would be rendered critical—but only for a time—for I expressed a firm conviction that as soon as the intelligence should reach England, countless British battalions would be fast poured into India to put down the revolt, when all who should be found to have stood by our cause and aided us in the hour of difficulty, would be rewarded. The Durbar officers had counselled the Maharana to concentrate his forces within the fortified gates of the Oodeypore Valley. Such a policy of isolation would have practically abandoned the Neemuch refugees to their fate. It would, moreover, have retarded the recovery of our position at Neemuch, which was attained through the aid of Oodeypore troops. His openly declared espousal of our cause, then, and immediate aid in troops, was all-important at that crisis; and these objects happily were secured before the Conference broke up. Practical effect was given to this momentous decision by His Highness' most trustworthy troops being placed at my disposal to take the field, accompanied by one of his highest and most trusted Chiefs, Bukht Singh, Rao of Bedla. Orders under

Khas rookha (the royal sign-manual) were at the same time issued calling upon all his loyal Chiefs and district officers to afford every aid in our operations, and to obey my orders as his own.

In the midst of these preparations, showing how urgent was the occasion, came intelligence on the 6th of the rise of the Neemuch brigade on the night of the 3rd. That it had come through native channels, unannounced to myself by any official or other communication from any authority or officer of the garrison, warranted the worst conclusions. Lloyd's unfinished express of the 2nd was the last to hand. Hastening despatch, then, the column was ready to march when two officers of the Neemuch force, Barnes of the Artillery, and Rose of the Infantry, rode into the Residency and reported that a party of over forty fugitives, women and children included, were gathered together at Doongla, a village about fifty miles distant, and bringing an express from Captain Macdonald, the senior officer of the party, describing their position as most critical and urgently calling for aid. Marched the same night in progress to the relief of the party, Barnes accompanying me, Rose being too exhausted with the fatigue of their long and anxious ride to take the field again at the moment.

An incident of the preparatory arrangements for taking the field may be here cited as at once illustrating a trait of Maharana Soroop Singh's fine character and conveying a lesson in Oriental diplomacy. On the Durbar Ministers calling to receive my instructions in virtue of the powers delegated to me by the Maharana, to my surprise Mehta Shere Singh, the late deposed Minister, accompanied them. As he filed in along with the others, I saw the situation at a glance. His Highness, reassured by my policy of strict non-intervention in disregard of the unconstitutional guarantee given by my predecessor to Mehta Shere Singh, as shown by the letter counter columned in the Supplementary Chapter, had voluntarily reinstated him specially to office to afford me the aid of the ablest man at his Court which the Mehtajee (as he was familiarly called), was admitted to be.

But before leaving the Capital it was necessary to take thought for the maintenance of general tranquillity in Meywar. To this end, in communication with the Maharana, I issued a Proclamation notifying to the recusant Chiefs that on my early return to Oodeypore I would enquire personally into their grievances, and that his Highness had promised to act on my counsel in each and every case, and advising them to rest upon my assurance and be patient. At the same time I warned all, that since general tranquillity in Meywar was essential at that juncture, any one, high or low, who ventured to disturb the public peace should be denounced as a rebel equally against the British Government as by his own Sovereign. But little practical efficacy, however, could be expected from mere words at a juncture when the power of corresponding action seemed remote and precarious. To assist the operation of this proclamation, then, I advised the Maharana to defer the final settlement of two important questions of succession to Chiefships pending at the time (viz., Amait and Bijolee) upon each of which respectively the most powerful Chiefs of the State were pretty equally divided; but so complicated were the relations of parties in the two cases, that Chiefs who supported the pretensions of the same claimant in one case, found themselves ranged on opposite sides in the other. Some of the most powerful Chiefs in the State, Saloombra, Deogurgh, Bheendur, Begoo, Gogoonda, found themselves thus situated—fortunately, in the interest of order, since by postponing the settlement of both questions in favour of either of the claimants respectively, parties in the State were held evenly balanced, and thus, as expectants, under a restraining influence. The Maharana followed my counsel in these two questions with strict unbending reserve, but in great self-denial of his personal predilections in favour of one of the claimants in each case.

A further precautionary measure to be taken had reference to the troop of the 1st Bengal Cavalry on detachment duty at Kherwarra, the head quarters of the Meywar Bheel Corps. As a wing of this 1st Cavalry formed part of the revolted brigade at Neemuch, the isolated troop could hardly be expected to resist the temptation to join their comrades in mutiny, if an opportunity offered. I was fortunate in having at Kherwarra, as Commandant of the Bheel Corps, and Superintendent of the Hilly Tract, that able officer, Captain, now Lieut.-General J. C. Brooke, and Captain, now Major-General R. M. Annesley,* second in command, holding respectively the official positions of 1st and 2nd Assistants to the Resident. By Captain Brooke's admirable arrangements the passes leading out of the Hilly Tract were closed, and the troop, under its gallant commander, Captain Ellice, was thus held in check.

Seeing that in view of the precautions taken their rising in a body was hopeless, they tried to desert individually, from time to time. But as often, the staunch little Bheels would be slipped after the fugitives, tracking them like blood-hounds, and invariably bringing them back prisoners.

The utter want of sympathy on the part of this contemned race of aborigines with the high-caste Hindoo or Mussulman of India exhibited by this incident, recalled a suggestion which I had submitted to Government in my official Inspection Report of this Bheel Corps in 1850, seven years previously, that a certain proportion of the aboriginal races should be eligible for enrolment in the ranks of our native army, when the distinction that good soldiers of these casteless races might gain on their military merits alone, would teach bigoted sectarians in our ranks that distinctions of creed did not enter into the composition of a disciplined soldier, whose

* Whose death, since the above was written, I have since seen with deep regret in the Military Obituary.—C. L. S.

highest religion should be his military duty. It goes without saying that had the suggestion in question, submitted at that early day, been adopted, the approach of the Mutiny would have found in the ranks of every regiment a few faithful among the faithless, to have warned their officers of the mischief that was brewing. On the final restoration of order the troop was disbanded.

The last and most important of the preliminary steps to be taken before marching from Oodeypore was to report to Colonel Lawrence the energetic measures adopted by the Meywar Durbar for the attack of the Neemuch mutineers, in having placed its troops under my command on taking the field, and calling upon all faithful chiefs and district authorities to afford every aid, on my requisition, in our operations. Indicating then a point, Sawar, in the north-east quarter of the Oodeypore territory, through which I proposed pushing the mutineers in pursuit, I ventured to hope that he would have a detachment of the European reinforcements from Deesa, which had been requisitioned among other precautionary measures before I left Aboo, moved to the point in question to intercept the retreat of the mutineers, when, between the European Column in front and my pursuing force in rear, with the Meena tribes of the Khirwar on their flank, their destruction, as an organised body at all events, might be confidently expected.

CHAPTER III.

RELIEF OF DOONGLA.

AND now, "To horse!" Our start having been thrown late in the night of the 7th June, by the necessary arrangements for ambulance for the women, children, and sick of the party of refugees, so urgently indicated in Captain Macdonald's letter, it was not till long after nightfall of the following day that we approached Doongla. We had halted for a few hours at Khyroda on the way, to feed and water the horses and ambulance cattle. No report of anything from the front had reached that town, situate about half way between Oodeypore and Doongla, so we proceeded on, cheered by the proverb that "no news is good news." Still, being aware that the mud walls of the village, undefended by guns or any other armament, could never resist an attack of the mutineers who we knew were scouring the country in all directions, it was not without feelings of anxiety bordering on pain that we rode forward—Barnes and the Rao of Bedla riding by my side at the head of our little cavalcade. The short twilight had faded into night and the darkness again had been lit up by the rising moon, throwing long shadows along the glades of the park-like scenery through which our track lay eastward, when about 10 o'clock the more than ordinarily dense foliage, denoting the site of an Indian village, betokened our proximity to Doongla. At the distance of about half a mile, then, we called a halt to allow of the ambulance to lock up in rear of the column. Ah, that *mauvais quart-d'heure* of suspense! Hours, days, months, years, hung upon the lagging minutes. No one spoke, but each read in the countenance of the other the "black care that was seated behind his own pommel." At length all being reported right in the rear, "Forward at a walk; march," was the word. Soon the grey walls of the village loomed into view: but all was still as death. Nearer, nearer, we cautiously advanced at a slow measured walk to guard against a surprise. Not a man of the enemy appeared in view—not a sound of horse, foot, or guns. Sweeping up then at a rapid trot under the walls, a feeble shout from the interior told that they had seen us, and the next moment Macdonald and Walker, Murray and others came rushing out of the gateway. "Thank God!" "Thank God!" was exclaimed and responded on either side as we met. The report of the Maharana's troops taking the field had preceded us, and had warned the mutineers to beat a retreat before the country was roused around them.

We found the refugees in the last stage of destitution, having escaped from the burning station with but their lives. Fatigue, anxiety, exposure and absolute want had done its work. Many were laid prostrate. The closeness and dirt of their confined retreat, in which cattle obtruded on the space allotted for the party, was causing sickness. Cholera had broken out. Davenport was lying dying. They could give no tidings of the rest of the fugitives from the station.

While the transport was being prepared for the conveyance of the party to Oodeypore, the women and sick were reposing in a range of low thatched huts, forming one side of the confined square. On the terrace in front of the huts I was sitting with the officers, gathering such confused accounts as they could give of the rising at Neemuch. One clear fact stood out in undisputed lurid relief—that at the signal of two guns fired by the artillery between eleven and twelve o'clock on the night of the 3rd, a general roar went up from all parts of the station, and in an instant every house was in flames. And now a touching incident of the situation occurred, serving to show that certain passages in our lives imprint themselves so indelibly on the memory, that even in sleep they move us as if waking, and waking, abstract us from surrounding objects, as if walking in a dream.

I was sitting, as I said, on the terrace with the officers listening to their several recitals of individual escape—the protection of two, in particular, by the people of an Oodeypore village against the mutineers on a point of honour, recalling the traditions of ancient chivalry, and the story of which will be told in its place—when our talk was suddenly arrested by a figure rushing in stooping posture out of the low-eavesed huts where the women were sleeping. On stepping out upon the floor of the terrace and standing erect, the now high-risen moon showed a lady in her white nightrobe. It was Mrs. Walker. Pausing for a moment to survey our group, she glided bare-footed, noiselessly and swiftly across the terrace, and throwing her arms around her startled husband's neck, gasped out in agitated accents, "Edward! dear Edward! the guns have fired." Alas! poor sufferer! The shock of that terrible incident, with its accompanying conflagration, had burned down upon her brain, and even in sleep recalled the fearful reality. Walker rose, reassuring her, and led her back to her trouble-tossed couch.

Short space, however, had the afflicted somnambulist to recover from the shock of her harrowing nightmare. The fierce morning sun of an Indian June demanded timely starting over-night. And here comes the Bedla Rao to say that the transport for the conveyance of his charge is all ready. Advancing to meet him, we walked out together to inspect the varied train ranged outside the walls to obviate confusion in setting off. There were palanquins for the women and children, and sick; pad elephants and horses for the officers and their servants; carts and camels for the luggage, &c. Nothing had been forgotten. How well that

ISLAND AND PALACE OF JUG MUNDIR,

IN THE LAKE OF OODEYPORE.

chivalrous Chief justified my confidence in fulfilling the charge I had confided to him to escort the party to Oodeypore, their safe arrival and convalescence of the sick, benefitting by the thoughtful arrangements made for their comfort, amply testified. How generously further the Maharana responded to my appeal in favour of the refugees is already known. The protection he extended to them was gratefully acknowledged at the time by His Excellency the Governor-General in a khareeta to His Highness' address, and afterwards by Her Majesty the Queen Empress, through her Secretary of State. A water palace on one of the beautiful Islands of the Lake was appointed for their residence, not less desirable as a secure retreat during the state of excitement at the Capital than as a pleasant and healthy abode. The gratified sense of safety and repose after all the dangers and trials they had gone through, was acknowledged by the refugees to have been enhanced by the cordial hospitality and personal visits of the Maharana. A report from my Assistant, Captain Annesley, who had been directed to proceed to Oodeypore to receive and remain in charge of the refugees, dated from the Jug Mundir Island Palace, may be here quoted: "His Highness, the Maharana, paid us a very handsome compliment by coming here in person yesterday in his state barge to ascertain that we were provided with every comfort. He asked to see the children, and to each he gave with his own hand two gold mohurs. In the evening they were taken over to the Queen's, when the Rana again sent for each two gold mohurs in his own name, and two in that of the Ranee's. In fact, nothing could excel his civility and kindness."

Before leaving the subject of the protection of the Neemuch refugees, I should be insensible if I did not take this opportunity of publicly expressing my gratification at the grateful acknowledgements tendered to me by the senior officer of the party, Major Macdonald, and the surgeon in charge, Dr. Murray, in the terms expressed in the subjoined letters, in recognition of the part which it was my good fortune to be permitted to bear in securing their safety:—

[PRIVATE.]

From Major (now Major-General) Macdonald,

Late Senior Officer of Party of Neemuch Refugees.

Dated 29th June, 1864.

To LIEUT.-COLONEL SHOWERS,

On looking back to our first meeting at Doogla, it strikes me that I and my "party" have not been sufficiently demonstrative in acknowledging our obligations for your prompt action in our behalf, to which may fairly be attributed the safety, *not* of *men* only, but the preservation from worse than death of the poor helpless women and children.

As Senior Officer whom you relieved by timely succour of much anxiety and responsibility, I accept blame for not having led those who deeply felt their obligations to you in making their sentiments known; but you must remember how at the time we were surrounded by dangers—how at once we separated in different directions, and how few of us have since met (of the whole body of refugees I have now the address of Dr. Murray alone). Poor Davenport, both my sergeants, and many others, are no more.

As now anything approaching a united expression of thanks to you is impossible, perhaps the acknowledgements of the officer then in command may prove acceptable if rendered on behalf of all those whom you rescued in that miserable village of Doogla, and I feel justified in this instance to speak for others, as the confidence your presence instilled in June, 1857, might be read in the faces of each man, wóman, and (I may add) child of my charge.

(Signed) J. MACDONALD.

From Dr. Murray,

Late Surgeon of Party of Refugees.

Dated 7th April, 1863.

In truth our party owe much to you and to the Rana. I, for one, shall not soon forget the joy that was infused into our people when you made your appearance at Doongla at the head of our faithful allies. It was a period of very great anxiety and suspense. Had the Rana gone against us, no power on earth could have saved us; and although there were brave hearts among us, determined to uphold the honour of England to the last, and to sell our lives dearly, yet the bravest among us shuddered at the awful fate that, under adverse circumstances, would have awaited our countrywomen and their little ones.

(Signed) T. MURRAY.

CHAPTER IV.

DETAILS OF THE MUTINY AT NEEMUCH.

THE following officers of the refugee party accompanied me as volunteers from Doongla in pursuit of the mutineers:—

Captain Sir John Hill, Bart., } 1st B. L. Cavalry.
" Ellice, }
Cornet Stapleton, joined at Neemuch, }
Lieutenant Barnes, Bengal Horse Artillery.
Doctor Murray, and
Staff Sergeants Supple, Nesbitt, Lane and Mellor.

Beating up for quotas of Horse at Burra and Chota Sadree, I directed the main body of my party to proceed from the latter post straight to Chitore, in the direct line of the rebel's retreat, myself riding round by way of Neemuch, accompanied by Barnes.

The charred and roofless walls of the fired dwellings stood out in harsh relief against the evening sky as we rode towards the ruined Cantonment, and as we passed through the silent streets the sense of desolation was heightened by the intelligence which had just arrived that the Mehidpoor Cavalry which was marching to reinforce Neemuch, had mutinied when within a few miles of the station, murdered their officers, Lieutenants Brodie and Hunt, and gone back to Mehidpoor to rouse and bring up the remainder of the Contingent.

I now learnt full particulars of the rise of the troops, one striking incident of which may serve to throw some light on the causes of the general revolt, in corroboration of my recorded view.

Resuming the narrative of preceding events above detailed from the correspondence of the Military and Civil officers in the station, it would appear that after Colonel Abbott had got the native officers of the Brigade to swear in his presence that they would remain faithful to their duty, he paraded the troops and informed the men of the oath their native officers had taken for themselves and on behalf of the men; then reminding them of the oaths they had themselves taken on enlistment, called upon all to stand firm in their allegiance. Hereupon a trooper of the Cavalry, by name Mahomed Ali Beg, stepped forth from the ranks and insolently addressing the officer Commanding, said, "What are our officer's oaths to us? Or even our own? Why should we keep our oaths to you who have broken your own? Have you not taken Oude?"

In the dead of that night, at the report of two signal guns, every house in the station was simultaneously fired, and while the startled inmates fled in wild affright for their lives, the ringing shouts of an infuriated soldiery proclaimed that yet another brigade, horse, foot, and guns, had passed from their allegiance to a Government charged with breach of faith, to swell the ranks of an organized rebellion.

The bazaar had for some days been nearly deserted in anticipation of the approaching event. The European residents fled in all directions through the night; the burning station and the destroyer behind, a wild and foreign country before and all around.

A noble attempt was made to save our position by Captain Macdonald, Commanding 7th Infantry Regiment, Gwalior Contingent, ably supported by his officers Lieutenants Rose, Davenport, Gurdon, and Doctor Murray. A wing of the regiment was on duty in the fort. Immediately on the Regulars rising, the other wing of this Gwalior Regiment was marched in under Lieutenant Rose, and then with his whole regiment within the walls, Captain Macdonald prepared to defend the fort. From the appearance of staunchness in this regiment while the regular troops of the brigade were supposed to be wavering, the fort guards had been detailed exclusively from its ranks; and certainly the marching into the fort of the wing outside at the command of its officers at the very moment when the other regular troops of the brigade had broken out into open revolt, seemed to afford a hope that this regiment would stand firm to their duty.

All Captain Macdonald's efforts however, during the long and anxious hours of that eventful night, proved of no avail. Though breaking out into no outrage the men at length told their officers that they could no longer obey them, and opening the gates implored them to fly and save their lives before the regulars came up. They then joined the general revolt, and the treasury being plundered, the whole brigade shared in the spoil.

Captain Macdonald and his officers on leaving the fort got separated in the *melée*, and fled in different directions. The lives of two of the party, Doctors Murray and Gane, were saved by the people of a neighbouring village of Oodeypore, under circumstances which recall the traditions of the rude days of the ancient chivalry, when the point of honour stood barbaric races instead of the vaunted higher motives of our later veneered civilization, and more than half redeemed their savagery. The first village these officers arrived at in their flight, was Kasoonda, of Oodeypore. Weary with their wanderings on foot, and exhausted by anxiety, they sought shelter and protection. The head-men of the village received them most kindly, gave them food, and a place to rest in. Their repose, however, was but of short duration. Within an hour or two of their arrival at Kasoonda, a party of the revolted cavalry galloped into the village and demanded the refugees. They had been sheltered in a small walled enclosure, where the head-men of the village resided. These reassuring their guests in the words of Doctor Murray's interesting narrative, "You have eaten with us, and are our guests, and now if you were our greatest enemy we would defend you,"—manned the walls, and refused to give up the officers. The soldiers threatened to bring guns, but nothing daunted, the villagers invoked the vengeance of their Suzerain, the Maharana, and maintained so bold an attitude that the mutineers were fain to retreat without effecting their vengeful object. At nightfall the head-men escorted the officers whom they had so nobly protected to the nearest military post of the Rana's, Chota Sadree, whence they proceeded and effected a junction with others of the refugees. "You have eaten with us and are our guests, and now if you were our greatest enemy we would defend you." Thus to the sacred obligation of the rights of hospitality in the barbarian breast, rights arising obviously out of a lawless state of society, when the protector of to-day might be himself a fugitive and a suppliant for protection to-morrow, do these two officers of the Neemuch garrison owe their lives.

My early public recognition of the conduct of the Kasoonda puttels by investing them with robes of honour (khilluts) in full Durbar, and the substantial grants of land by which the Maharana of Oodeypore at my instance rewarded the good service towards our Government performed by his subjects, have already been duly reported. Government further on its own part, in pursuance of its expressed intention to reward the faithful, bestowed a substantial money-reward on these meritorious men, and placed, in the construction of a well at Government expense, a lasting and useful monument in Kasoonda, of at once the noble conduct of its head-men and the gratitude of the British Government.

Doctors Murray and Gane were the last upon whose fate doubt hung. All then had escaped the immediate danger of the rise of the troops, except the wife and two children of Sergeant Supple of the Artillery, who were unfortunately massacred before the poor woman could effect her escape from the lines. The sergeant himself, a brave and good non-commissioned officer, was doing his duty at the time in aiding his officers, Lieutenants Walker and Barnes, in the attempt, desperate under the circumstances, of suppressing the signalled revolt. It was not until these gallant officers were fired at by their men that they gave it up.

CHAPTER V.

PURSUIT OF NEEMUCH MUTINEERS.

IT had occupied me but a few hours to gather the above details, when leaving at Neemuch, in attendance on the Superintendent, Captain Lloyd, a confidential Durbar officer, who had control over the Raj troops at the neighbouring Meywar posts, and having been joined by Lieutenant Stapleton, 1st Bengal Cavalry, who volunteered for the pursuit, we rode on to overtake the party which had been ordered to march straight to Chitore.

On passing Neembahera *en route*, where it was known the Neemuch mutineers had halted two days, I sent for the head official of the place, Bukshee Gholam Mohee-ood-deen Khan. He came out, attended by a troop of armed men with lighted matches, himself holding a pistol in his hand, while answering evasively the questions I put to him. On joining the party which had marched straight from Sadree upon Chitore, I learnt that in passing Neembahera, they found the gates closed against them, and had to pass the heat of the day,—the season being the hot winds in June,—under the scant shade of trees outside the walls of the place.

Arrived at Chitore, having marched then about 120 miles in four days, we found ourselves immediately on the line of the mutineers' retreat. Just beyond, at Gungrar, we learnt that a party of the cavalry had been there but an hour or two before we arrived, hunting for the postal runners at the station. Arrangements were made for the protection of these, and for the security of the post in transit. Continuing the pursuit without halt, stragglers began now to fall into our hands. Among others the two Meywar Agency chuprassees, who had been left in charge of General Lawrence's property at the Agency, and who had joined the mutineers after plundering the same, were overtaken and captured. Property of various descriptions strewed the road of the retreating rebels.

In reference to the complications at Neemuch, occasioned by the claim of the Gwalior Wakeel to recover possession of the Jawad-Neemuch districts on behalf of his Sovereign in consequence of the revolt of the Neemuch Brigade, a brief historical retrospect is necessary in explanation.

The Jawad-Neemuch districts had originally formed an integral portion of the Oodeypore territories. During the incursions in Rajputana of the combined forces of the Mahrattas and the Pathans, the latter under Ameer Khan, in the early part of the present century, the Jawad-Neemuch districts had been occupied by and finally ceded to the Mahrattas; while certain other districts, Neembahera, Serong,

Tonk, &c., had been occupied by Ameer Khan. During our war with the Mahrattas, it being an object of policy to detach Ameer Khan from his league with the Mahrattas, he was offered by the British Government, in pursuance of the Roman maxim, "divide and govern," the sovereignty in and over all the detached portions of territory then in his possession. He closed with the offer, and was installed as Nawab of Tonk, the principal of the captured provinces then in his possession, eight in number. Thus, out of this dominion of spoil, was created the principality of Tonk. Administered as were the isolated districts comprising the same by semi-independent Amils, or Governors, we shall see by-and-by, in the complications ensuing, the defect of an arrangement so inherently devoid of healthy centralization. Most of the detached districts of this Mahomedan principality sympathised with the Delhie dynasty during the Mutiny, and gave trouble. The Jawad-Neemuch districts had been assigned over to the British Government in course of the arrangements dictated to the Gwalior Durbar after the successful campaign of 1843, to provide for the due and punctual payment of the Gwalior Contingent force. The mutiny of the Contingent Brigade of all arms at Gwalior, as also of the Contingent Regiment of Infantry at Neemuch, afforded a plausible pretext for intrigues on the part of the Gwalior Wakeel, for recovering possession of the assigned districts on behalf of the Durbar.

The adoption of extreme measures towards that functionary was indicated by the Agent Governor-General; but since all apprehension on the score of integrity of territory had been obviated by our recovery of the station of Neemuch and occupying it in force, I reported that I proposed to formally dismiss the Wakeel, and request, through the Resident at Gwalior, that another might be appointed to replace him. This was to obviate the risk of the Gwalior Durbar taking offence.

I may here transcribe extracts from my Progress Report of the 12th June, dated from Chitore, which may serve to give a general view of affairs in Meywar at that juncture:—"Having found many ladies and children in Fort Neemuch, the families of officers who had fled in a different direction from Oodeypore on the night of the mutiny, I expressed my view to Colonel Abbott, commanding the station, and Captain Lloyd, the Superintendent, that they ought not to be exposed to any further risk, but sent to join the party at Oodeypore, and I ordered an escort to be held in readiness to conduct them. It was anticipated, however, that the ladies would not go. Leaving the delicate negociation in the hands of those gentlemen I proceeded on, after but a few hours' stay in Neemuch, accompanied by Stapleton, who had gallantly volunteered for the pursuit, to overtake my camp here (Chitore), arriving last night. This morning, however, the intelligence from Malwa in reference to the mutinied Mehidpoor contingent is of so dark a complexion that I shall write to urge that the wishes of the ladies may not be consulted in a matter of such moment to their safety, and that they may be forwarded to Oodeypore under the Durbar escort told off for that duty. This source of anxiety being removed I shall be more at ease in following up the fast-retreating mutineers. A few more of our late marches, by which we have done some 120 miles in four days, must soon bring us up with them. I am most fortunate in being associated in the pursuit with a body of officers who enter thoroughly into the spirit of the thing, and go through all the fatigues and privations of such service at such a season of the year with admirable fortitude and cheerfulness. As the Nusserabad dâk (post) appears to be open, pray let me hear from you as to whether we may reckon on your sending any force to obstruct the progress of the mutineers through the Ajmeer district. If you can send us out some tea it will be most acceptable. Direct to Kekree, with which post we will communicate, and which, indeed, it will be advisable to occupy, as the rebels must pass pretty close to the town and may plunder it." "P.S.—There are no guns in the fort. I led Colonel Abbott to expect that I would get two nine-pounders which are attached to the Oodeypore troops moved in; but the intelligence now received indicates such political complications that the step of allowing Meywar to occupy the Neemuch fort with guns might give umbrage to the Gwalior

Durbar—a result which at the present juncture might occasion serious aggravation to our general difficulties. I would beg to suggest then that you let me have two nine-pounders from the Ajmere magazine. If you can forward them to Bunaira I will detach a party to receive and escort them to Neemuch. Let me hear, please, on this head, outside dâk, to Bunaira. European gunners, if only a couple to accompany the guns, would prove of great use. All quiet internally in the Meywar State."

I wrote on the same date (12th June) to Captain Lloyd, Superintendent Jowad - Neemuch districts, urging that the measure of the removal of the ladies and children to Oodeypore should be carried out without delay. Further, that an European officer should be appointed Postmaster and to have all native correspondence read before delivered, adding, "I will take the responsibility of officially sanctioning the measure, or any other that Colonel Abbott and yourself may jointly consider expedient, and will write to Brigadier Macan at Nusseerabad suggesting the adoption of a similar measure of precaution at that post." This measure, I may here remark, on being reported, was followed up by the General Order issued by the Government, No. 1,456, dated 29th July, 1857, authorizing "the chief Covenanted Civil or Military Officer at every station throughout India to assume, until further orders, the office of Postmaster, or to assign the office to any other

Covenanted Civil or Military Officer at the station."

The following letter to Brigadier Macan, commanding at Nusseerabad, refers to the proposed combined attack on the mutineers.

(Dated) CAMP SANGANEER,
15th June, 1857.

"MY DEAR BRIGADIER,

I have arrived thus far with a force of Meywar troops in pursuit of the Neemuch mutineers, and we march to-night to Shahpoora where we shall be within a forced march of them. They are marching *viâ* Kekree, as I informed Colonel Lawrence by letter a day or two ago. I had previously written to him before leaving Oodeypore, on the 7th inst., to say that I proposed pursuing the mutineers, and should be ready to co-operate with such trustworthy Meywar troops as I could collect if he should think proper to move the Nusserabad Brigade to intercept them in their passage through the Ajmere district. Not having received any reply from Colonel Lawrence, and concluding that he is not in your neighbourhood, I think it right to submit the proposal I made to him for your consideration, and would beg the favour of an immediate answer. As the mutineers are marching daily, the question does not admit of delay. The vital importance of striking an effective blow on this body need not be dwelt on. . . . Even should the mutineers have passed Kekra before you could move to the attack, a hot pursuit would certainly disorganise them, and their guns, at least, fall into our hands, jaded as the cattle must already be by the hot pursuit I have carried through Meywar. . . . I have had great difficulty in keeping the post open, as the mutineers had organised a system of cutting off the runners. As these men have to thread their way through the jungle tracts in disguise their packets should be in the smallest possible compass." Suggesting, in conclusion, the appointment of an European Post

Master, as adopted at Neemuch, to give us control over the native correspondence and to reduce the bulk of the packets for selected essential despatches.

(Signed) C. L. SHOWERS."

On same date and place I addressed the following letter to Colonel Lawrence—

MY DEAR COLONEL,

I write a line, on the chance of its finding you at Nusserabad, to say that I have written to Brigadier Macan on the subject of the proposal I submitted to you before leaving Oodeypore, and again while *en route* a day or two ago, for attacking the Neemuch mutineers. I hope you may have sent instructions to the Brigadier so that he may be prepared to act. Even if not in time now to take up a position ahead of them, a hot pursuit would soon disorganise them, and the gun-cattle being jaded from the pursuit through Meywar, the guns, at least, ought to fall into our hands. I can supply some thirty camels and three elephants to assist in mounting the Europeans. I shall await the Brigadier's answer at Shahpoora. . . . We have overtaken and seized the two chuprassees who carried off your property. The house was a sad scene of ruin, everything broken. The coachman took off your horses. Your loss has been, I fear, exceedingly heavy. Pray let me hear from you at Shahpoora.

The Raos of Humeergurh and Mowah, both loyal Meywar chiefs, received us well in passing through the capitals of their chiefships, and joined our party in person with their respective quotas of horse.

At Shahpoora, however, a chiefship holding possessions both under the Meywar and Ajmere, and owing a divided allegiance therefore equally to the British Government as to the Maharana of

Meywar, we experienced a change of wind. Found the gates of the fort closed, no *peshwai*, no supplies. We had heard that the mutineers had halted here. The report of the battle of Budla-ka-Serai, before Delhi, which arrived just at that juncture, effected an instantaneous change in the attitude of the Shahpoora people. I was not aware at the time of how prominent a part my lamented Brother had had in that action. It was magnified by rumour into the fall of Delhi. And similarly magnified, it may here be observed once for all, was every report, good or bad, that almost daily floated upon the wind throughout the critical period of the rebellion; each success before Delhi gave us in remote parts the temporary advantage of a retrieval of our position; while, on the other hand, each disaster anywhere—and how many and fast following and terrible they fell—was knelled as a final catastrophe, and tended to complicate seriously the difficulties of our situation.

We had now (the 16th) arrived within a forced march of the rebels, but no communication from the Officiating Agent Governor, Brigadier-General Lawrence, had reached me conveying the expected instructions regarding the combined plan of attack on the mutineers, which, as above stated, I had submitted for his consideration by express before taking the field at Oodeypore, on the 7th. In that letter, I had indicated *Sawur* as the point in the Ajmere district through which, I was of opinion, from my knowledge of the country, the mutineers would pass. They passed through and halted at the very place. I subsequently addressed the Agent Governor-General, again by express on the 15th from Sanganeer *en route*. No preparations, however, having been made to intercept the mutineers, or to cover the military station of Deolee, lying a few miles beyond the proposed position to be taken up at Sawur, the mutineers had passed on unopposed and burnt Deolee, after seizing two pieces of ordnance and the whole magazine in store there. A staff-sergeant with ten women and children left at Deolee, had had to fly for their lives, and having been rescued by the Oodeypore authorities of Jehazpoor, were brought into my camp.

Proceeded straight from Shapoora to Jehazpoor, marching by day in expectation of intercepting the revolted Mehidpoor Cavalry, which Corps, 600 strong, we had certain information from Neemuch, had passed at some distance from that Station, making northward *viâ* the Mandulgurh route, and ought by calculation to be approaching our line of march.

Saw nothing of them on the march, but the next morning intelligence was brought to us at Jehazpoor that this body of mutineers has crossed our line of march but a few hours after we had passed, and had proceeded *viâ* Sawur, to effect a junction with the Neemuch mutineers who had waited for them at Deolee.

I was still without any communication from General Lawrence, nor did any force appear to be approaching from Nusseerabad.

Extract of a letter from Brigadier-General Lawrence, dated Nusseerabad, 16th June, 1857.

"However much I desire to strike a blow against the mutineers with the Troops here, I do not feel myself justified in running any risk in the present state of national feeling, and the destruction of the mutineers is to me very secondary to the preservation of Ajmere, which, I am quite sure, would fall were we to move from this, to say nothing of the immediate rise of the country which would ensue."

At length, on the 20th, an answer was received definitively negativing, as will be seen by the appended extract from General Lawrence's letter of the 16th, my suggestion for a combined attack on the mutineers on account of the risk of Ajmere rising if the force were to move from Nusseerabad. The same express brought me an answer from Brigadier Macan, dated the 18th (copied in Appendix), written after communication with General Lawrence, and concurring with his superior in regard to the operation in question on precisely the same ground. There remained no alternative then, after having carried the pursuit without halt to the frontier post of Meywar, accomplished moreover through the hot winds in the month of June, by day marches for the most part under a burning sun, with not a tent among our party,—no alternative left but to allow the Neemuch Brigade to proceed on to Agra unmolested.

In submitting suggestions for an attack on the mutineers I was influenced by the following considerations, which, I had hoped, might have weighed with General Lawrence to dispel the apprehension of Ajmere rising in the event of the force being temporarily moved from the vicinity to secure so great an object, viz.:—As Ajmere had not risen, nor attempted to rise, nor had any disturbance in the district broken out during the whole month immediately succeeding the first crash of the rebellion at Meerut and Delhi, on the 10th and 11th May, although there was not a single European soldier not only at or near Ajmere, but not in the whole of Rajputana, and notwithstanding the strong incitements to insurrection offered by the revolt of the Nusseerabad troops in its immediate vicinity on the 20th May, and of that of the Neemuch Brigade on the 3rd June,—if with such opportunities and incitements to rise, Ajmere had remained quiet throughout the first eventful month which saw our seemingly immovable power so rudely shaken, why should it have been assumed that that city and district would infallibly rise after the British European Troops had appeared on the scene if they should be temporarily moved to a short distance in pursuance of a vigorous strategy, which in itself might have appeared calculated, judging by the sedative effect produced by vigorous action elsewhere, to hold the inhabitants in awe. Further, although there is a Mahomedan shrine of great sanctity at Ajmere, yet the Mussulman community, comprising some six or seven hundred families, which subsist upon the wealthy landed endowment of the shrine, and from which community at such a period of religious excitement, danger might under ordinary conditions have been apprehended, lay from the very circumstance of their ample means of subsistence in the land, under a powerful restraining influence. Isolated as this Mussulman community was in the heart of Rajputana, it seemed to me as very improbable that they would commit themselves, and risk their secure livelihood by rising against our Government unless their cause had conclusively triumphed at Delhi, and support from their co-religionists was at hand. Again, the population of the city of Ajmere being mostly Hindoo, including great numbers of wealthy merchants and bankers, the instincts of such a class might be expected to range them with their followers on the side of order as opposed to anarchy.

The immediate advantages that might have been expected in my opinion to flow from attacking the mutineers, as proposed, were the probable disorganization and dispersion of the Neemuch and Mehidpore mutineers in detail; the saving of the British Station of Deolee with its ordnance, magazine, &c., and especially as the warning the fate of these mutineers would have presented to the secretly disaffected in the several Stations in Central India, which afterwards rose, Mhow, Indore, Augur, &c., and in all others lying far removed from the principal seat of the rebellion, Delhi—to all such the example might have operated as a deterrent. A letter from Durand now before me, dated Indore, 29th June, 1857, describing his critical position there, concludes with these words: "I wish Lawrence had struck a blow;" words evidently wrung from him in bitterness of heart in clear apprehension of the brewing storm that burst upon him but two days later. On the other hand—reversing the picture—by the Neemuch mutineers being suffered to pass openly through the country unchallenged, without a blow being struck at them by the British power directly assailed in its highest imperial interests, not only were these probable advantages lost; but the disaffected throughout the country were encouraged by the apparent abandonment of the position and prestige of a ruling power involved in such tacit acquiescence in the mutiny of our troops, to join the movement which seemed in the ascendant, and at any rate, safe. Thus when the Neemuch Brigade marched from the plundered station of Deolee, it represented with the Mehidpoor Cavalry, which had there joined it, and its additional trophy guns, a formidable military force invested with a prestige that was calculated to conciliate support to its ranks. On then it rolled, gathering as it went.

At Tonk, the capital of the Mahomedan principality of that name—a dominion of spoil as above described—the mutineers were cordially welcomed and entertained, and joined by a large body of the population of that place, soldiery and other. Thus reinforced the mutineers marched upon Agra; and it was only on this formidable band of the insurgents appearing before the Capital of the Government of the North Western Provinces, that the Kotah contingent, stationed at Agra at the time, and which had stood true for nearly two months of the insurrection, revolted and joined the mutineers.

The Agra Garrison marched out on the 5th July, and gave battle to the rebels, but was compelled, mainly by the fire of the Deolee guns, to retire within the walls of the Fort, leaving the assailants in full possession of the Station, Military and Civil.

The Capital was laid in ruins. The Lieutenant-Governor with the whole garrison shut up within the walls of the fort. The jail burst open and thousands of desperadoes let loose upon the world.

With this accession of strength in numbers and prestige the Neemuch mutineers joined their brethren in rebellion at Delhie, to give as might be expected under the circumstances, that support and impetus to the movement that urged the three days' vigorous attack on the British position on the 14th, the 18th, and 20th July, by which Brigadier Wilson lost the services of hundreds of men of his already slender band, and was placed for the time on the defensive.

CHAPTER VI.

SALOOMBRA, THE CHIEF OF THE BARONS.

WHEN the attack on the Neemuch mutineers by the proposed combined operation had been conclusively abandoned it only remained for me to return southward to provide for the safety of Neemuch, and to take measures to hold in check the disaffected Chiefs of Meywar. The principal of these seemed disposed to take advantage of the revolt of the British troops as a favourable opportunity of carrying their points against their Sovereign, or breaking out into open rebellion to set up, as was threatened, a rival to the throne.

Having received intelligence that the remaining arms of the Mehidpoor Contingent, Infantry and guns, were about to follow the revolted cavalry, which had come up through the Mandulgurh pass, we marched, on returning towards Neemuch, by that route in the hope of intercepting them. The report however proved unfounded.

After closing and occupying that pass, then, I visited the Rao of Begoo in passing homewards, and bespoke the active co-operation of this Chief. How well he has responded to the call is proved by his occupying and holding for us the frontier British posts of the tract under the Neemuch Superintendency, formerly his own possessions, on the occasion of the general revolt of the British district authorities, when the rebel Mundisore Shahzada claimed their allegiance. In recognition of this important service, Government has since bestowed a Khillut on the Begoo Chief.

See report No. 108, dated 14th April, enclosing Neemuch Superintendents.

On return to Neemuch the general insurrection had made such head, and the aspect of affairs around this isolated post was so threatening in view equally of the attitude assumed at that juncture by the recusant Chiefs of Meywar, as of impending irruptions of rebels from without, that it was deemed expedient to remove the party of women and children of the refugees left at Neemuch to a place of comparative safety as indicated by the presence of European troops. The Saloombra Chief, indeed (the head of the faction) had gone so far as to threaten open rebellion for the object of deposing the Maharana and setting up a rival to the throne at the ancient Capital, Chitore, if His Highness did not at once accede to all his demands; a term even was fixed, eight days being specified as the limit of his forbearance. The serious complication occasioned hereby may be inferred from the measures which Sir Henry Lawrence had thought it necessary to recommend to the adoption of Government in his case in view of the contumacious and defiant bearing o this Chief even in presence of our full power anterior to the Mutiny. The measures in question were distinctly set forth in para. 13 of the Agent Governor-General Sir Henry Lawrence's Report of the 5th February, 1857, and comprehended the displacement of the Saloombra and Bheender Chiefs from their Chiefships through the employment of two strong columns of British troops, and their banishment from Rajputana. How rising rebellion in Meywar was kept down at the juncture in question by my counsel to the Maharana on the one hand to stand firm, and my pregnant warning to Saloombra on the other, was fully reported in my letter No. 27 of 30th January, 1858. The incident may be here briefly related as introducing a perhaps not uninteresting episode.

The Chiefship of Saloombra is the most powerful of the sixteen principal fiefs of the Oodeypore State. The Rajput Premiership, or dignity of Military Minister, as distinguished from the office of Civil Minister, being hereditary in the family, the Rawat of Saloombra is invested with certain special privileges. For instance, when a Rana of Oodeypore leaves the capital, he has the government of the city and charge of the palace during his Highness' absence. By his hands the Sovereign is girt with the sword, and from him he receives the mark of inauguration on his accession to the throne. Saloombra leads, by right, the van in battle, and in case of the siege of the capital, his post is the *Soorug-päl* (the Sun Gate), and his residence the fortress that crowns it. Another of the recognised privileges of the feudal tenure under which the Rawats of Saloombra hold is, that on the succession of a new Chief to that principality, the heir-apparent to the Oodeypore State should proceed in person to Saloombra to perform the mutual ceremony of "girding on the sword," and conduct the new Chief to the capital to be formally invested. Now, since at the period in question, the Maharana Soroop Singh having no son, there was no heir-apparent when Rao Keseri Singh succeeded to the principality of Saloombra, the Maharana proposed to depute the highest Chief at his Court (the Rao of Bedla) to proceed to Saloombra to perform the ordinary ceremony. But to this arrangement the proud Keseri Singh objected, and demanded that, in the absence of an heir, the Maharana himself should proceed in person to Saloombra to conduct him to Court for investiture. This demand was held by the Maharana to be preposterous, and as such was rejected. Hence the recusancy of Rawat Keseri Singh. Some of the other Chiefs, moreover, had more legitimate cause of grievance against their Suzerain, because of his desire to commute the service of their retainers into money payments—an innovation on feudal usage affecting their dignity. This grievance Rao Keseri Singh shared in common with his compeers: consequently at the juncture in question the league of recusant Chiefs which he headed constituted a source of danger to the public peace in Meywar, in view of the temporary weakness of the paramount power through the outbreak of the Mutiny. The incident in question, then, had reference to the demand of the Saloombra Rao for the personal proceeding of the Maharana to Saloombra to conduct him to Court—reiterated at this conjuncture with a threat that, if still refused, he would set up a rival to the Gâdee (throne) at the ancient Capital of Chitore, in the person of a scion of a collateral royal branch—a term of eight days being given for compliance. The Maharana sent this ultimatum on the part of his rebellious feudatory to me by a confidential messenger, seeking my counsel.

I saw at a glance that the scheme was well planned. The historic associations, at once proud and mournful, clustering, like its native ivy, round the beetling battlements of the isolated hill fortress of Chitore, surmounted by the lofty *Kirtrustromb* (column of victory), towering into view for miles around, were well calculated to lend prestige to the movement, as recalling to the warlike "children of the sun" (*Sunea Mookee*) the glories of their ancestors centring in that spot. "There is a sanctity in the very name of Chitore," according to the Meywar tradition, "which from the earliest times secured her defenders." Its mournful memories, again, recalling the terrible disasters which ultimately occasioned the change, between three and four hundred years ago, in the seat of Government from the isolated hill fortress of Chitore to its present sheltered site, Oodeypore, nestled at the base of the Aravulli Mountains, would equally serve to kindle emotion and soften the heart to receive whatever impression might be sought to be imposed by the designing. The Ranas of Oodeypore had rendered themselves peculiarly obnoxious to the jealousy of the Mahommedan Emperors of Delhie by the independent attitude they, alone of all the Rajput princes, assumed in refusing to give a daughter of their house in marriage to the royal bed. They had thus to endure successive invasions from the affronted Suzerains to the last and final catastrophe. Peerless Pudmani! Proud yet sad, at once, thy fate!—destined

> 'Like another Helen.
> To fire another Troy!'

and thyself to perish in the flames! But let me tell the tale as 'twas told to me, and bespeak the sympathy of my readers for as heroic and sad a legend as Romance ever wove out of Fancy's fairy web; yet true withal, as attested by the ruined battlements and crumbling palaces amidst which the scene is laid.

Seated with the venerable bard amidst fallen columns in a secluded nook by the brink of the Zenana Bath, excavated out of the solid rock, in full view of the dark mouth of the subterranean passage leading up to the *Zenana*, recalling the legend—the old man, with eyes alternately flashing fire and anon melting into tears, as the strain of his story modulated between the major and minor keys of heroic effort and innocent suffering, thus began:—

CHAPTER VII.

"BY THE SIN OF THE SACK OF CHITORE."

IT was towards the close of the 13th century—in the year 1275. The fame of the beauty of Pudmani—"fairest of the fair," as her name imports—had reached the Imperial portals of Delhie. The Emperor Alla-o-deen sent to demand her surrender. She was the daughter of Hamir Sank (Chohan) of Ceylon. Bheemsi, uncle of the reigning Rana, Lakumsi, and Protector during his minority, had espoused Pudmani. To him, therefore, the demand of the Emperor came. The stereotyped haughty answer of the Sesodias to all such demands for the daughters of their princely house was returned.

Again the fertile plains of Meywar were ravaged by a Tartar horde. Again the isolated hill fortress of Chitore was invested, and the comparatively slender garrison besieged by a far greater proportion than the threefold excess prescribed for the operations of modern warfare. Like vultures thronging to the prey, the numbers of the invaders were virtually illimitable.

But the defenders of the fortress were the flower of the Meywar chivalry. After years of fruitless siege the Emperor Alla-o-deen was fain to restrict his demand to a mere sight of this extraordinary beauty, and acceded to the proposed compromise of beholding her through the medium of mirrors. Knowing he could trust to the honour of a Rajput, he came but slightly attended, and, having gratified his wish, returned. The Rana's courtesy led him to attend his temporary guest to the foot of the fortress. Here the faithless Pathan, in anticipation of the Rajput's trustful honour, had an ambush laid. Bheemsi was made prisoner, hurried away to the Tartar camp, and his liberation made dependent on the surrender of Pudmani.

The garrison was struck with consternation at this fell treachery of the Pathan. "What was to be done?" The Princess came to their relief. She would go as a ransom for her lord. Having provided herself with the means of securing her honour, she called in council two chiefs of her own kinsmen of Ceylon, her uncle Gorah and his nephew Badul. A wife's affection and a woman's wit had devised a scheme for the liberation of the Prince, without hazarding her own life or fame, which met with their approval. Intimation was despatched to the Emperor that on his raising the siege, the fair Pudmani would be sent in a manner befitting her dignity and his exalted station, accompanied not only with the ladies and handmaids who would attend her to Delhie, but also with those who would wish to pay their last respects to their departing queen. The sanctity of female decorum and privacy would, of course, be secured by royal command from the intrusion of vulgar curiosity. Accordingly, no less than seven hundred covered litters proceeded to the royal camp. On arrival they were set down within the extensive kanats (canvas-walled enclosure) surrounding the royal tents. The Prince Bheemsi having been liberated, half-an-hour was granted for a parting interview with his departing bride.

And the King reclined on a crimson brocaded ottoman in his gorgeous tent hung around and carpeted with the choicest shawl produce of the Cashmere looms, the entrance leading under an emblazoned canopy supported by gilded tent-poles. But little he now heeded such gorgeous surroundings of royal state. Love levels all. Pudmani in a cottage were worth all his palaces and all his seraglios. His erotic thoughts dwelt with ecstasy on the beauteous form that had been reflected in the mirror, and he revelled in anticipation in the amorous embrace of such transcendent charms.

Meanwhile, the Prince Bheemsi mounted on horseback had been permitted to leave the camp on return to Chitore.

The camp gong strikes the hour. The time is up. The King counting the lagging moments and listening with bated breath for the signal, springs up with outstretched arms, as if already clasping his dearly won prize in his embrace. When—instead of his coveted Pudmani, forth springs from each litter a

PALACE OF RANA BHEEM AND PUDMANI,

IN CHITORE.

Chitore chief armed *cap-à-pie*, backed by the six armed soldiers who had been disguised as his litter-porters. Pursuit was ordered. The devoted band perished to a man in covering their Prince's retreat. A fleet Arab had been provided, mounted on which Bheemsi galloped up the paved causeway leading to the fort. The clatter of the horsehoofs of the pursuers was heard at the portals as the Prince bounded through, when, the gates being slammed to, a shower of missiles hurled the pursuers back to tell the tale to their discomfited king.

Draw the veil over the renewed honeymoon of the rescued Prince with his fair and gifted bride. The accompanying picture represents the water palace on the mountain lake of Chitore, consecrated to their joys. There let us leave them for a while—in dreaming blissful oblivion of the nightmare of the Past; all unconscious of the rude awakening of the Future.

Alla-o-deen foiled in his object, and admonished by the havoc made in his ranks, joined to the dread of further determined resistance, abandoned the enterprise and retired his army to Delhie.

The King sat on the Peacock Throne--but gloom reigned in the Imperial halls—King of Delhie, and Emperor of Hindostan in virture of his extensive conquests over the most ancient and most powerful principalities within its limits; the King-Emperor Alla-o-deen, assumed the proud title of Secunder Sani, or the Second Alexander, and impressed this effigy on his coins. With every apparent concomitant of pomp and circumstance to ensure happiness, he was ill at ease. A secret canker was growing at his vitals and poisoning the springs of life. His Majesty dispensed justice, according to custom, in the Dewan-i-Aum (public hall of audience). The routine business proceeded; but the King's eyes were fixed on vacancy. Matters of urgency succeeded, imperatively demanding the royal orders.

An express from the Governor of Ghuznee reporting a revolt of the Ghilzais and urgently calling for reinforcements.—"*Dâkil Duftur.*" (Let it be filed.)

The Soobahdar of Oude reported a raid of the Nepaulese and plunder of the treasury.—"Let it be filed."

The Chief of Police of Delhie reported the discovery of a conspiracy to blow up the palace and set up a Hindoo rajah.—"Let it be filed."

The Chief Eunuch reported a revolt of the harem in consequence, and the *Zenana* portals thrown open at night.*

"*Ba chushm-i-Pudmani! che muzaika.*" By the bright eyes of Pudmani! What does it matter? The King rose: the Durbar was closed.

"What words are these," the people said to one another as they streamed out, "Is the King gone demented?" An ominous whisper ran through the hall, and spread through the bazaars of Delhie.

---

* The ordinary device adopted by the ladies of a Seraglio of showing dissatisfaction with their lords.

From the carved fretwork screen of the balcony pavilion of the palace overhanging the river Jumna, a careworn face was seen gazing intently down upon the smooth mirrored surface of the limpid stream. But it gave him not back the reflection of the face that he sought, to reassure him by visible lineaments that he was not possessed by a phantom, and to exorcise the spectre. In vain. The mirrored face still haunted his dreams by night, his thoughts by day. And ever the pang of disappointed desire rose to his mind, sharpened with the maddening humiliation of the defeat his arms had sustained. Himself a sufferer in spirit for the first time in his wayward life, all the evil deeds he had done, all the carnage and havoc which he had inflicted in his unprovoked invasions, rose to the king's mind to sting him with the pangs of remorse. At night the ghosts of his victims passed in weird procession by the side of his trouble-tossed bed, each recounting the deed of death done in his case, and as erst to the third Richard, crying:

> 'Let me sit heavy on thy soul to-morrow;
> Despair and die!
> Dream on, dream on of bloody deeds and death,
> Fainting, despair; despairing, yield thy breath!'

After convulsive tossings as each successive apparition passed in turn, the king at length started up in wild affright and rushing out upon the terrace of his dormitory, found himself beneath the star-bespangled sky before he awoke to a consciousness that it was nothing but a dream—shadows—shadows all. Still mirror-haunted, he thought to find distraction in the illuminated *sheesh-mahal* (looking-glass chamber), in the superstitious hope that amidst the myriad reflections given back by the kaleidoscopic mirror-fractured surface of which the walls around and the glistening roof above were wholly composed, one reflection, if only one amongst the myriads, would give him that of the face he had seen mirrored at Chitore. He looked with eyes straining, starting from their sockets. Blinded with the glare and agonized with disappointment, he covered his eyes with his hand and sank exhausted on an ottoman. Starting up suddenly after a while, as a happy thought struck him, he laughed a derisive "Ha! ha! Have I not a hundred such?" The King sought refuge then in the Zenana to woo wonted solace from sensual gratification. The silken shawl-hung screen yielded noiselessly to his extended hand. Entering softly, the dim voluptuous light of Chinese lanterns revealed the fair forms of the beauties of the Court, all seeking in jealous rivalry to win a smile from their lord. In vain. Life had lost its zest. Lust, satiated by possession, burned fiercely alone for the forbidden! And is not this the history of the sin of the world from the beginning? Eve had her apple—Alexander his yet unconquered world—Alla-o-deen his Pud-mani. And each and all of us, what? Ever a crumpled rose leaf in the downiest bed—an *aliquid amari* in the sweetest cup,—recalling the poet's reflection :—

> "Qui fit Mæcenas ut nemo, quam sibi sortem,
> Seu ratio dederit, seu fors objecerit, illa
> Contentus vivat."

But this could not last. The King was going melancholy mad. The skilfullest hakeems were called in. One prescribed one nostrum, another another—all equally in vain. Till at length a palace intrigue, fomented by the resentment of the neglected Begums, eventuated in a Court conspiracy to displace Alla-o-deen and set up a rival to the throne. This coming to the Emperor's ears, recalled him to a sense of the situation, and rekindled in all its fury the original tiger in his nature. Love, or her fallen sister Lust, gave place to Revenge. "Yes, Pudmani shall yet be mine, though but to grace the conqueror's car: while Chitore—hateful name! shall be laid in ruins, and be henceforth to the world—but a Memory!"

Again the clang of preparation rings through the arsenals of Delhie. Again forced war contributions are levied throughout the Empire and the revenue collectors commanded to apply the screw to replenish the treasury, exhausted by the previous war. Alla-o-deen having thus recruited his strength, marches south again at the head of a countless host. Again the fertile plains of Meywar were overrun as by a swarm of locusts. Again the fortress of Chitore was invested; on this occasion so completely and in such force that, as the chronicler figuratively put it, "not even a bird could have passed out."

This second siege began in the year 1290, and lasted ten years. It would demand the pen of another Homer to recount the deeds of daring done in this second siege of Troy. I can but recur briefly to the closing scene. Why dwell on the long drawn-out privations and hardships heroically endured by the devoted and daily dwindling band around Rana Bheem, before the final, fatal truth forced itself upon him—that the defence could no longer be sustained? Eleven of his brave sons had fallen, and it only remained to secure the safety of the last, Ajeysi, so that his line should not become extinct, before devoting himself for Chitore. A contest hereupon arose between the Rana and his surviving son: but the father prevailed, and Ajeysi, in obedience to his commands, with a small band passed safely through the enemy's lines by night and reached Kailwarra, in the Aravulli Mountains, in safety. Rana Bheem, then, satisfied on this point of lineal succession, called his Chiefs around him, and donning saffron robes, the emblem of martyrdom, prepared to throw open the gates, and, sword in hand, rush upon the foe, and thus 'die for Chitore.' But another awful sacrifice was to precede this act of self-devotion in that horrible rite, the *Johur*, where the females are immolated to save them from dishonour or captivity. The subterranean passage leading up from the Zenana Bath to the palace was the scene of this terrible sacrifice. The defenders of Chitore, standing aside mute and motionless, beheld, 'in long procession led,' the Queen, their wives and daughters, all of female youth or beauty that could be tainted by Tartar lust, to the number of many thousands, slowly gliding towards the fatal cavern. Last in the sad procession walked Queen Pudmani, with measured steps and slow—hands clasped across her breast and eyes fixed upon the ground. One last look she cast on her now deserted home of the water-palace, the scene of so much bliss—one upward glance to Heaven, as sinking involuntarily on one knee with clasped hands upraised, she mentally implores, "Must it be?" Towards her husband, standing like a carved statue, petrified with grief, in front of the mute and motionless band, she dared not look. Another moment, and, last of the doomed, she has disappeared in the dark recesses of the yawning cavern. Faggots are piled at the mouth—the torch applied. The flames rise, the welkin rings with shrieks! Hear it not, brave Bheem, or 'twill unman thee for the last act! Think only of the faithless wretch who seized thee by treachery, that he might ravish thy wife as thy ransom—think of the awful death that he has brought upon her by his revenge! Let such thoughts nerve thy arm in the last onslaught, and, cutting a human lane with thy sword, if thou canst get within striking distance of the perfidious king, strike home—and thou'lt die happy! The gates are thrown open—

the Rana calling upon his devoted clans, for whom life has no longer any charms, they descend the paved causeway to the plain, and with a reckless despair, rush sword in hand upon the foe, carrying death and meeting it in the overwhelming ranks of Alla-o-deen.

The Emperor, conqueror at last of this fateful fortress, rode up and entered it with mingled emotions. He found himself master of an inanimate capital, strewed with the bodies of its brave defenders. But SHE—the innocent cause of all this havoc—the fair Pudmani! where is she? Whether the later-nourished revenge, or a revival of his earlier mirror-inspired passion, dominated the question, what boots? The smoke yet issuing from the recesses where lay consumed the once fair object of his desire, is all the answer that this mortal world can give.

Since that devoted day the cavern has been sacred. No eye has penetrated its gloom; and Superstition has placed as its guardian, a huge Serpent, whose 'venomous breath' extinguishes the light which might guide intruders to the 'place of sacrifice."

To this day the most solemn adjuration of the Sesodias is: "By the sin of the Sack of Chitore;"* and the numerals 74½, which represent the number of *manis* weight of cordons of distinction taken from the necks of the Rajputs who fell in the last assault, are

* "Chitore marya ra pâp."

tilác, or accursed—recalling the similar incident of Hannibal, on gaining the battle of Cannæ, measuring his success by the bushels of rings taken from the fingers of the Roman Equites who fell on that memorable field. To eternise the memory of the disaster at Chitore, the numerals in question are banned,—74½, marked on the banker's letter in Rajasthan, is the strongest of seals, for the 'sin of the slaughter of Chitore' is thereby invoked on all who break open a letter under the safeguard of this mysterious number.

If the steps of the Western traveller should ever carry him to Chitore, let him ascend the Kirtis-tromb,* and from its summit mark the desolation of the scene. Not an image of female loveliness, nor carved statue erected to the brave and noble, has escaped the 'defacing fingers' of the great Iconoclast. Descending and turning his back then on the ruins, on every fallen stone of which is engraved in imperishable lines the names of Bheemsi and his hapless bride Pudmani, let him recall the legend which I have endeavoured so imperfectly to recount, and standing at the gateway of the fortress, look down in imagination on the countless tents of the investing Tartar horde, and invoking the Genius of the place, join in the solemn adjuration: "By the sin of the Sack of Chitore!' †

* Column of Victory.

† "Chitore marya ra pâp."

CHAPTER VIII.

SALOOMBRA CRISIS AND ISSUE.

REVOLVING thus in my mind the eventualities of Saloombra's adroitly devised scheme, and recognising in its possible success, danger to our weakened position, I yet thought the best course in the present, as it will be found generally in all cases of danger, was "to grasp the nettle." So telling the Maharana's confidential officer to return with my advice to His Highness to dismiss Saloombra's messenger summarily without deigning any answer, and that I would write to him, I addressed myself to do so.

"MUSHFIKA! My Friend," I wrote, "a somewhat incredible rumour has reached me,—that oblivious of the traditions of your princely house and dishonouring the tombs of your ancestors, whose conspicuous loyalty has from time immemorial constituted them the pillars of the State of Oodeypoor, you contemplate rebellion against your Suzerain. I cannot believe it. I cannot believe that a Chief who has so princely a domain, would recklessly risk its forfeiture by allying himself with houseless vagabonds for the most part (*kana ba doz*)* in creating a disturbance. Nevertheless, I think it my duty, as the British representative in Meywar, to warn you that any one, be he high or low, who attempts to disturb the public peace

* Literally, carrying their house on their back

in Oodeypoor at this juncture, when general tranquillity is essential to all, will be denounced as a rebel against the British Government equally as against his own Sovereign. I need hardly add that from your commanding influence in and over the hilly tracts in your vicinity, you could not expect to be absolved from responsibility in the event of any disturbance arising in the hilly tract, especially in the neighbourhood of Kherwarra."

I despatched this missive by a special messenger to the Rawat. The last sentence I added on account of a report which Captain Brooke, Superintendent of the Hilly Tract, had sent me, that Saloombra was instigating an attack on his post, Kherwarra, and that the state of affairs was critical. On my informing Brooke of the purport of my letter, he wrote, in forwarding for my information copy of a written report he had received regarding the Rawat's attitude, dated the 24th June, 1857: "Two days after this letter was written, the Rawat must have received yours, which will bring matters to a crisis, and he will have to make up his mind. The Wakeel here" (Kherwarra, where dated) "thinks an outbreak is certain, and emissaries of Saloombra are about."

It did bring matters to a crisis. In due course I received a reply from Saloombra, "assuring me that I had only done justice to his unwavering loyalty, and that nothing was further from his thoughts than the course indicated by the injurious rumours which had reached me,—a device of his enemies." Thus the impending danger from that source was averted.

CHAPTER IX.

HOLKAR AND SCINDIA.

ON the eve of the departure of the party of officers of the Neemuch mutinied regiments for Nusseerabad, intelligence was received of the revolt of Holkar's troops at Indore, on the 1st July, attended with the massacre of most of the European inhabitants of the place,—the escape fortunately of the Agent Governor-General, Colonel Durand and his staff, only appearing by subsequent accounts. Together with this intelligence came that of the rising of the troops simultaneously at the contiguous station of Mhow, when the Cantonment was burnt, and the Commandant, Colonel Platt, and other officers killed.

The rebellion having thus spread to the contiguous province of Malwa, to the south, and Meywar lying in the direct route of the mutineers and insurgents of Indore and Mhow to Delhi (the principal seat of rebellion to which the rebels from all parts directed their steps), the contemplated despatch of women and children from Neemuch, in the absence of any escort of Europeans or reliable troops, became a question of anxious solicitude. It only remained to trust in the difficulty to the support and protection of the Oodeypore Durbar, whose active efforts in equipping troops for the field for the pursuit of the Neemuch mutineers had already been so satisfactorily exhibited. Calling upon the Durbar, then, to provide an escort, the party was consigned to the protection of the Durbar officer in command, and notwithstanding the increased sources of danger arising from the events of the period, were safely escorted to their destination through perhaps one of the wildest tracts of country in India, held at all times precarious. Colonel Abbott, the senior officer of the party proceeding to Nusseerabad, wrote on arrival there under date the 17th July: "The commander of our escort, and the escort, have behaved admirably." The route *viâ* the Mundulgurh pass had been adopted to avoid Neembahera, through which the ordinary route lay, on account of the doubt regarding the friendly disposition of the head man (Bukshee Gholam Mehee-oodeen), which had been raised in my mind by the favourable reception on the one hand which the Neemuch mutineers had met with in passing through that place, and the hostile attitude on the other assumed by that functionary towards my party when in pursuit of them.

At the time when this party of the Neemuch refugees were escorted by the Oodeypore troops through dangers of no ordinary magnitude to a place of safety, the other party, who had been rescued at Doongla, were residing in safety and comfort in the water palaces of the Oodeypore lake under the protection, and as the honoured guests of the Maharana of Oodeypore. They were afterwards safely escorted by His Highness' troops across the Aravalli Mountains to the summer retreat of Mount Aboo. Thus, through the staunch fidelity and friendship of our ally the Maharana of Oodeypore, the whole of the refugees from the flames of their desolated dwellings at Neemuch, and from the fury of the revolted soldiery, were rescued and escorted to places of safety.

Reverting to Neemuch, the chief danger there to the stability of our position at the period in question arose more from political causes than from the probability of attack from mutineers. For the Neemuch district surrounding this isolated Military post being held in assignment under treaty by the British Government on account of the expense of the Gwalior Contingent, a question arose on the successive revolt of all arms of that Contingent at all the posts where they had been stationed, how far the British Government was entitled to retain possession of these assigned districts.

The calm discussion of this question was endangered by an impression which the Superintendent of Neemuch appeared to have imbibed, on the one hand, that the Gwalior Wakeel accredited to the Meywar Agency was intriguing, or had intrigued to supersede him in his jurisdiction, and had even compassed his life; and by an impression, on the other hand, which the Gwalior Wakeel seemed to have entertained that it was our intention to abandon Neemuch and make it over to Meywar.

The ground for the above impression on the part of the Superintendent would appear, from Captain Lloyd's letter to my address of 5th June, to have been the circumstance of the Gwalior Wakeel having initiated measures for the preservation of order, and conducting the Civil duties of the district after his (the Superintendent's) retreat on the occasion of the revolt. Speaking of his hopes of getting back to Neemuch and relieving the Gwalior Wakeel through the aid of the Meywar Hakim of Chota Sadree, where he was at the time a refugee, Captain Lloyd writes, "there has been a deep game played about this. I am doubly fortunate in having got away. A party of twenty-five 1st Cavalry were chasing me all yesterday, and had I been put out of the way the assumption of authority by the Gwalior Wakeel in a district belonging to his sovereign would have been a justifiable measure perhaps under the circumstances, and once established not easily got rid of."

The cause of the Wakeel's misapprehension, on the other hand, was probably our sending away the women and children, the officers of the mutinied Regiments leaving at the same time; and further, the presence of a considerable body of Meywar troops which I had assembled to maintain our position and order generally, may have created doubts with regard to our ultimate plans.

From whatever cause arising, however, the mutual misunderstanding between the British Superintendent and the Gwalior authorities in regard to the assigned districts had produced a very unsatisfactory state of affairs on our Southern Frontier, the station being threatened continually with inroads from the neighbouring Gwalior post of Mundisore, which kept the people of the bazaar and town of Neemuch in a succession of panics.

The removal of this misunderstanding would have been rendered utterly hopeless had I followed even in spirit the instructions for extreme measures towards the Gwalior Wakeel which were sent for my guidance at this juncture by General Lawrence and referred to in my despatch to Brigadier-General Lawrence's address dated 27th August, 1857. The marginally appended extract from General Lawrence's letter will serve conclusively to illustrate the spirit in which his instructions were conceived.

Extract of a letter from his Assistant Lieutenant Impey under instructions from Brigadier General Lawrence, dated Beawar, 11th June, 1857.

"He (General Lawrence) hopes that if the Gwalior Wakeel has done as people say, you will have hung him ere this."

The breach, however, with the Gwalior authorities in these remote parts of Scindia's territory would have been the least of the evils entailed by such a course. The inevitable open rupture between Scindia's Durbar and the British Government which must have ensued was a contingency, the disastrous consequences of which at that conjuncture it is impossible to over-estimate.

When, then, the last remaining Brigade of the Gwalior Contingent rose at Augur on the 8th July, killing two of their officers, Lieutenant O'Douda and Doctor James, as also a lady, Mrs. James, and the Gwalior Wakeel thereupon raised the question on the part of his Durbar touching the restoration to Scindia of the assigned Neemuch districts, the complication, in view of the state of feeling subsisting as above described between the Superintendent and Gwalior Wakeel, threatened to become serious. The question of relinquishing territory at such a juncture was not to be entertained for a moment, as involving an admission of weakness which would have been fatal to our prestige. The subject of the transfer, then, was at once and authoritatively quashed by me in my public Durbar where it was raised, as reported in my letter dated 27th August, 1857. The Gwalior authorities were invited, however, at the same time to join in our defensive arrangements for the maintenance of the district against the rebels, as assumed to be equally of the Gwalior as of the British Government—a mark of seeming confidence that reassured the Gwalior authorities on the subject of our present intentions and ultimate plans in regard to the Neemuch province. Their reviving confidence was further strengthened by another measure taken simultaneously, viz., the breaking ground in progress of the construction of some projected field works round the fort. This was a palpable indication that so far from abandoning, we were resolved to keep the post for ourselves. Rumours of coming inroad, previously so rife, then died away, the post through Malwa was again opened, and confidence restored in the bazaar.

In view of the formidable attitude of armed neutrality in which Gwalior then stood with the whole of the revolted contingent (8,000 of the best disciplined and equipped Native troops in India) at the Maharajah's absolute control, besides his own numerous Lushkur troops—His Highness uncontrolled and unfettered, further, by the presence of the Political Agent accredited to his Court, who had had to leave Gwalior and take refuge in the Agra fort, together with all the surviving officers of the contingent—it seemed an object of especial moment to maintain this power in a state of friendly neutrality so favourable to British interests. To this end, accordingly, my policy was consistently directed especially throughout the period of our critical relations with the Gwalior authorities in the presence of the Mundisore (Malwa) rebellion as on the occasion above referred to. In the absence from their posts of the Political Agent accredited to the Gwalior Court and of the Agent Governor-General Central India having supervising control over it, together with his Political Staff—all swept away from their posts by the storm of the rebellion—my action, as the only political officer holding relations then with the Gwalior State through the Maharajah's Wakeel accredited to the Meywar Agency, seemed urgently called for. The result is now patent to the world; but the success of my policy was early felt, for Captain (now General) Nixon, writing from Fort Agra, 6th August, 1857, expressed the views of the Lieutenant-Governor when he said: "The Gwalior Rajah is the best friend we have. He is doing the best he can to prevent the mutineer troops in his country moving out of it."

The considerations of high state expediency by which my policy towards Gwalior was guided at that critical period, gathered force in an accelerating ratio from the circumstance of the sister Maharatta state of Indore being placed, by internal insurrection and military revolt, precisely in a similar position relatively to our Power, and prompted the action I took towards this State also, at the same conjuncture, when its young ruler was left without the counsel and support of the British Political Officers of the Central India Agency consequent on their retreat from the capital.

On the intelligence of the insurrection at Indore and mutiny simultaneously at Mhow on the 1st July, reaching me at Neemuch, Holkar's Wakeel, accredited to the Resident for the Meywar States, emphatically disavowed, on the part of his master, all prior knowledge of the coming events of which Indore had become the scene, and expressed His Highness' reprobation of the same. In regard,

That I did not err in my judgment of Holkar's real bearing towards us at a period which seemed to justify universal distrust, and when appearances at first view seemed against him, was conclusively proved by his subsequent course, as emphatically testified to by the Agent Governor-General, Sir Robert Hamilton, in his parting address appended in margin. The correctness of my judgment in weighing Maharajah Holkar's conduct at that dark hour of doubt has been further established since the preparation of this report, by the high authority of His Excellency the Viceroy and Governor-General (vide his Khareeta to Maharajah Holkar's address dated Delhie, 16th January, 1860), wherein the Governor-General conveys to His Highness the "thanks of the Queen's Government for his loyal co-operation and support he had given to the British Power during the late convulsion in Hindostan and especially on the occasion of the insurrection at Indore."

"I am glad to take this opportunity of stating publicly and emphatically that to your conduct and deportment during the late disastrous period are to be attributed the tranquillity and good order which have been preserved in your territories, and that my Government are deeply indebted to you and Maharajah Scindia for the example you set and the admirable manner in which you have behaved throughout. No one can tell the increase of mischief that would have occurred, had there been any hesitation on your part and I am confident that at no distant period my Government will suitably express its approbation and sense of your services."

Considering the formidable and absolutely unfettered attitude of the sister Maharatta State of Gwalior at the same conjuncture, and the fact of the lesser States under the Indore Agency, Dhar, Amjhera, &c., having already taken part against us, it was of course of the last importance to save Holkar being thrown into opposition by the difficulties by which he was surrounded, much aggravated naturally by the suspicion with which he was regarded by the British representative, Colonel Durand, who after his retreat out of Malwa had, I believe, closed for the time all correspondence with His Highness. My impression at the time in this regard has since been corroborated by the following passages from the 1st vol. of Malleson's History of the Indian Mutiny. Being dedicated to Sir Henry Durand, it may be presumed to have been written in full knowledge of his sentiments on the point in question. In referring at page 62 to the attack on the Residency by Holkar's troops and the Maharajah's protestation that "this act had been committed without his sanction or authority," the author states, "Durand himself never believed this." Again, in the following page, in speaking of the impression produced in Holkar's mind by Durand's attitude towards him, he says, "He (Holkar) knew in his heart that Durand had condemned him." Again, at page 83, in speaking of Durand's official visit to Holkar after the disarming of his troops on the 14th December, Malleson adds: "It was the first time since the month of June that Durand had seen Holkar. Regarding him in his own mind as an accessory to the attack made upon the Residency on the 1st July, Durand had sent a report of all the circumstances of the case to Lord Canning, and pending a reply, had declined to renew personal relations with a prince who might possibly be adjudged by the English authority in India to be a rebel."

Colonel Malleson proceeds to pronounce judgment, *ex cathedrâ*, on the point at issue, in the following terms*:—"Looking at the question as a whole, I am of opinion that Holkar was free from complicity with the mutineers,"—a sagacious discovery, truly, to have made a quarter of a century after the question had been definitely set at rest, both by the emphatic testimony borne by the permanent Agent Governor-General, Sir Robert Hamilton, to his conduct and deportment during the disastrous period of the insurrection, and especially by the formal letter addressed to the Maharajah by the Viceroy, dated 16th January, 1860, quoted in the preceding page. Malleson proceeds in his summing up, reviewing the circumstances, "Whilst then Holkar must be acquitted of complicity with the rebels, the conduct of Durand in refusing to hold confidential intercourse with him until the Government of India should clear him from the suspicions attaching to his conduct, must be upheld and justified."

---

* Vol. 1, page 233.

Right or wrong as a question of abstract ethics, I fear it can hardly be denied that the practical tendency of such a course in holding suspended so long over the Maharajah's head a charge of so grave a complexion as to affect, in its issues, not only his throne, but even his head, was possibly to drive the young prince to desperation, and throw him into the arms of his fellow-countrymen in rebellion, Nana Sahib, Rao Sahib and Tantia Topee. The actual result in keeping all Western Malwa in an agitated state, and thus endangering the peace of the neighbouring districts, was felt by General Sir Richmond Shakespear, Resident at Baroda, who expressed his sense of the embarrassment in his letter of the 9th August to my address. As combining a calm, judicial view of the situation at this juncture, with a fine appreciation of Durand's distinguished personal qualities, the letter now before me may be usefully cited :—

"BARODA, *9th August*, 1857.

"All is perfectly quiet here, and I hope will remain so, but much will depend on what Durand does at Indore. I learn that on the 1st he was with the Bombay Column at Simrole, one stage apparently from Mhow, that Holkar's troops were still mutinous, and that he called for aid from us. Durand is a clever, resolute man, but I am surprised that he went to Asseergurh to bring up the Bombay Column instead of going direct to Mhow as Colonel Stockley did. The latter arrived there on the 25th, and it strikes me that had Durand gone at the same time he might have greatly strengthened Holkar before the Bombay Column arrived. I fear Holkar's people saying that Durand is coming to destroy, and not to strengthen Holkar. A victory even over the latter would in our present state, be a misfortune. But Durand is doubtless right, and there must be circumstances with which I am unacquainted. What makes me so interested in it is, that all Western Malwa is kept in an agitated state until the question with Holkar is settled. Hutchinson is still at Mhow, and as far as I know, there is no one at that very important post (to Goojerat) Bhopawur."

Durand's own account of the attack on the Residency, written to the Nawab of Jowra, dated 13th July, 1857, from Hoshungabad, may be appropriately added here :—

"MY DEAR NAWAB,—Major-General Woodburn's advanced troops being close on the Nerbudda I shall soon be at Mhow with them, and I only write a few lines to thank you for your letter of the 4th inst., and to acquaint you that we retired with our two guns and the few horse and foot who were true to us without loss. During the attack by Holkar's guns and troops we only lost a few horsemen, horses, and gun bullocks. It was the defection of the Contingent Infantry which forced us to withdraw. They had an understanding with Holkar's troops and would not do their duty, and had the Treasury in their hands.—I remain, my dear Nawab, yours very truly (signed), H. M. DURAND."

A Maharatta league against the British, of Gwalior, Holkar, and the Maharatta leaders of the rebels, Nana Sahib and Rao Sahib, to restore the kingdom of the Peshwa, was a contingency, the remote possibility of which, at the opening of the rebellion, had advanced to the bounds of speculation in view of the half-compromised situation in which the young rulers, Scindia and Holkar, found themselves placed by the insurrection of their troops against the British, the massacre at their respective Capitals of British subjects, and the absence of the British representatives from their Courts. Such a complication it was obviously of the last importance to avert.

How far the action I took, as the only Political Officer left in official relation with these two Maharatta States, through the Agents accredited to me from both, tended to maintain both the young Princes, Holkar and Scindia, under extraordinary temptations, in that state of open neutrality and secret friendly co-operation which has proved so favourable to British interests throughout the most critical period of the rebellion, the foregoing historical review may enable a judgment to be formed.

CHAPTER X.

SECOND MUTINY AT NEEMUCH: RINGLEADERS SEIZED AND EXECUTED.

AT the time of the risings in Malwa above referred to (the beginning of July), we were but nine Englishmen, officers and staff sergeants included, present at Neemuch, our only reliable force at the post being Meywar troops. Yet even these our enemies tried to turn against us, by circulating a report that we were bent on destroying their caste equally with that of our own native troops, and had for this purpose mixed human bone-dust in the flour served out to them. On hearing of this machination, I sent for the Oodeypore Durbar officers in attendance on me, and mentioning the circumstance, looked to them to put the matter straight. They proceeded at once to the lines of the men, accompanied by the Residency Wakeel in attendance, by name Urjoon Singh, a Brahmin. Arriving at the bazaar, they asked for the suspicious flour to be produced. Urjoon Singh, taking up a handful, ordered it to be kneaded and made into a chupattie, and ate it before their eyes. This at once dispelled all doubts; of such efficacy is the magical imprimatur of Caste! By its influence in this instance a real danger was averted.

Besides Meywar troops, some Kotah Raj Contingents, too, were present, against my protest as a source of danger, and they soon began to show signs of that hostility to the British which was crowned not long afterwards by the murder of the Political Agent, Major Burton, and the occupation of the Fort of Kotah in open rebellion. For the defence of our post, then, I applied for guns and a party of Europeans to hold the Fort. One Company of H. M.'s 83rd Regiment and two guns were sent from Nusseerabad, but along with this welcome reinforcement Brigadier-General Lawrence, who was then in Military Command as well as Political Chief in Rajputana, sent, against my wish, a Detachment of Bombay Native Regulars, Cavalry and Infantry. These soon exhibited signs of the prevailing disaffection as, being recruited for the most part from kindred classes and the same districts as the Bengal Troops, might have been foreseen in view of the similar circumstances under which they would find themselves at Neemuch. Again the Station was agitated with all the premonitory signs of another mutineer crisis. Night after night the bare blackened walls of the houses destroyed in the first conflagration were lit up by the glare of burning out-offices, stacks of grass, everything inflammable. Again the bazaar, frightened by renewed rumours of impending risings, began to be deserted. On the

23rd July, three of the 83rd were wounded in a street row, and their lives only saved by the individual gallantry of Lieutenant Barnes, Bengal Horse Artillery, and Lieutenant Thackwell, late 15th Regiment Native Infantry. These officers while playing at rackets heard a commotion in the street. Proceeding to the spot with their revolvers they used them with such effect as served to hold at bay the armed assailants of the surrounded soldiers. The disturbance was at once suppressed, as reported in my letter, dated 23rd July, 1857, but it coming out afterwards that a general rising had been planned on that occasion which the Bombay Regulars were to have joined, and having moreover received information that the foiled assailants only awaited an accession of strength in the expected arrival of a further reinforcement of Native Regulars, which was under orders by Brigadier-General Lawrence to march to Neemuch, I thought it right to recommend strongly the countermand of the further reinforcement, and did so through my despatch of 1st August, 1857.

My warning was, however, disregarded. The result was only what was to be expected. The second night after its arrival (the 12th August) a general rising and contemplated massacre of all the Europeans was planned, and on discovery of the plot, only frustrated by Colonel Jackson, Commandant, marching down the detachment 83rd Foot into the native lines at night previous to the appointed hour, and seizing the ringleaders. This was not effected, however, without the loss of an European killed and others wounded including an officer.

A third attempt made two days later (on the 15th idem) was suppressed with equal promptitude and success. A reliable body of Oodeypore troops forming my body-guard was always present to co-operate when necessary in the preservation of order.

Though one expressed object of my recommending the countermand of further detachments of Native Troops to Neemuch, viz., to guard against the force there feeling itself strong enough to break away and reinforce the rebels at Delhie,—had been overlooked in the rejection of that recommendation, it seemed doubly necessary to provide against such a contingency when the arrival of the reinforcements had precipitated a mutiny. Though suppressed, the Native troops were yet in such a condition that the men were nightly deserting with their arms, and the troopers with their horses too. The precautionary measure that suggested itself was to move the Native troops from their lines to within the entrenchment I had had constructed round the Fort. It was supposed that the attempt would be resisted. By none was this view more decidedly entertained than by Brigadier-General Lawrence, who in conveying the same to me expressed his opinion that it "would make them break out into open mutiny at once." The measure was decided upon, nevertheless, as indispensably neces-

Vide his letter No. 43, dated 27th July, 1857.

sary to give us a command over our Native troops. The Native Cavalry and Infantry were marched down by successive divisions, by different roads, and at intervals—the Company of the 83rd, our two 9-pounders, volunteer troop of gentlemen and Meywar Horse, under myself, being under arms to support the operation. Colonel Jackson's dispositions were admirable and completely successful. Not a division resisted. Then with the whole of the Native regulars secured in an entrenched Camp under the guns of the Fort, and double sentries at the one single gateway, mutiny was hopeless, and desertion impossible. There, under the guns, with port-fires lit, were executed three of the ringleaders in the recent risings before the eyes of their comrades, all under arms. Not a man stirred. Not a murmur in the ranks. Our command over the men was complete.

CHAPTER XI.

THE MALWA INSURRECTION.

ABOUT this time (the middle of August) a fresh insurrection arose in the contiguous province of Malwa, which soon acquired formidable dimensions; and being headed by a fanatic Priest Prince, by name Feroz Shah, who preached a crusade against the British, an attack on Neemuch was imminently threatened.* The origin and progress of the movement which, working through the Mahomedan element in the population of Mundisore, established the Shahzada as Ruler there, on the overthrow of the Gwalior authorities, are fully described in my report dated the 7th September, 1857, and may be here briefly summarised.

About the period in question, a wandering Hadjee, calling himself a Shahzada, prince of the Delhie house, made his appearance at Katchrode, near Mundisore, a town of Gwalior situate thirty miles south of Neemuch. Raising the flag of religion (Deen ka Jhunda) he preached a crusade (Jehad) against the British. The governor of Mundisore marched with a small force to quell the disturbance, found no

* Corroborated at page 65 of Malleson, Vol. III.

difficulty in doing so, and turned the Hadjee out of Katchrode. He took refuge in an obscure temple in the vicinity, called Burmajee ka Mundir.

Here in his obscure retreat the holy man reçeived the homage of thousands of devotees, who thronged to show their sympathy for their spiritual pastor in his misfortune. As the numbers swelled, that sympathy assumed the dangerous form of a desire to establish the Shahzada in a worldly kingdom, in pursuance of which the assembled host of devotees, in number about two thousand, responding to the Jehad that had been proclaimed, openly raised the standard of rebellion and marched against Mundisore in progress to Neemuch and Delhie. The Shahzada's appearance before Mundisore was the signal for a general rise of the Mahomedan population of the town and district containing some ten thousand Mewatees, and of the defection of the Mukranee and Vilaetee mercenary troops of the Soobah. The chief Gwalior authorities of Mundisore, the Komasdan (Civil Governor) and Kotwal (Chief of Police), in endeavouring to suppress the revolt, were wounded and taken prisoners; a third officer of the Soobah was killed. The Kotwal, a Brahmin, was made a Mussulman of. The fact of such a rite, ordinarily performed upon unconscious infants as their baptism into the Mahomedan faith, being practised upon an adult, in annihilation of the faith of his fathers, may afford an illustration of at once the cruelty and intolerance of the leaders of the movement. Another instance of much greater barbarity will have to be detailed further on in the narrative, by the exigency of historic truth, and which I fear will shock the sensitive with its unparalleled grossness combined with cruelty. A general assault was then made on the Barah (government house,) the treasury plundered, records burnt, and the Shahzada being brought in triumph was seated on the gádee (throne) and proclaimed king under a royal salute.

May it be permitted to the profane historian, in recognition of the universality of the relation between cause and effect obtaining in the moral world equally as in the physical, and, comparing small things with great, to draw hence a lesson for the Catholic Church. Does the incident of this Priest Prince bowing in submission to physical force, and voluntarily retiring to a humble temple retreat, and thence, through the effective sympathy of his followers, emerging to overthrow the government of his persecutors in the seat of their temporal power, furnish any analogy to the case of the Papacy under similar recent persecution? How much more dignified would have been the attitude of Pope Pius IX., if, when forcibly dispossessed of his temporal kingdom, he had left Rome, shaking the dust from off his shoes, and retired to some humble sanctuary, saying with his great Master: "My kingdom is not of this world, but of God." Would not the whole Roman Catholic world, penetrated to its lowest depths with infinite sympathy for the head of their Church in his martyrdom, have banded themselves in a crusade on his behalf?*

Recurring to the insurrection at Mundisore, a certain Mahomedan called Mirzajee, was appointed Purdhan (Chief Minister.) This person, from all I learned of his antecedents, would seem to have been much concerned in instigating at once the insurrection against the Gwalior State, and movement against the British. The farmer-generalship (Ijaradar) of the Mundisore district was hereditary in his family for about a century; but the office was abolished and the district taken under Khalsa (State) management about twenty years before the insurrection in question. The Mirzajee was, perhaps, deluded into a belief, from the insurrection at Delhie, that the Mahomedan rule was to be restored. Be that as it may, the branch of the dynasty set up at Mundisore would appear to have had no misgivings as to its permanence. Proclamations were issued to all the neighbouring Princes and Chiefs, claiming their allegiance and calling upon them to present themselves. Thus the Rajah of Pertabgurh, Nawab of Jowra, Chiefs of Rutlam,

* *January 23rd.*—I would submit whether the above comments, penned weeks, are not invested with a peculiar significance, by the intelligence from Rome flashed by telegraph last night, reporting the Pope's speech of Saturday, on receiving a deputation of German nuns. "I rely," said Leo XIII., "on the influence of all the Catholic people to solve the present insupportable position, and to enable me to regain the Temporal Power which is essential to the prosperity of the Church."

Seeta Mhow, and others received such missives, which were duly forwarded on for my information. Saloombra also received a threatening letter, Capt. Brooke wrote me, for not attacking Kherwarra; as well as Doongurpoor and the Bhoomia Chiefs for giving us assistance.

But whether the Shahzada, or his appointed minister, was directing the movement, the power undoubtedly lay in the hands of the soldiery and armed insurgents. The terms of the proclamation, which was promulgated by beat of drum throughout the city simultaneously with the installation of the king, left no manner of doubt on this head. It is characteristic of such armed insurrectionary movements universally, as illustrated by the action of the Pretorian guards in Ancient Rome; of the Sikh Khalsa in the Punjab; of the Jannesaries in Egypt, among others, and runs as follows:—

"The Creation is God's,—
The Country is the King's.
Authority belongs to the paramount Soldiery!"*

The determined hostility towards us of the Shahzada and his followers at Mundisore was evinced, from the first, by the systematic method in which they cut off our communications to the South. Not only was the Government Post absolutely

---

* "Khalluk Khoda ka,
Moolk Padshah ka,
Hakumat Sipah bahadur ka!"

closed, but our private couriers (kossids) were waylaid and killed. The movement, as might be expected from its origin, soon got beyond the control of the originators, as may be gathered from the terms above cited, in which the new kingdom was proclaimed by beat of drum.

They were bent on mischief. Some of the Mundisore Fort guns were equipped as field artillery with the openly declared object of attacking Neemuch. Colonel Durand, Agent Governor-General, Central India, wrote to me in French cypher, and extract from his letter was appended to my despatch under date the 22nd January, 1858, para. 9, that "he had been advised by letters from Nagpoor, from Hydrabad, from Surat, from Bombay, from Gwalior, and from intercepted letters, that a general insurrection was planned to take place in Malwa." The anonymous letter to his address dated 29th August, 1857, which Colonel Durand considered of sufficient weight to transmit to Government for publication (vide Dhar B. B. 8th April, 1859), stated, that one declared object of the Mundisore Shahzada was to drive the European troops from Neemuch.* The

* "On m'avise par lettres de Nagpoor, de Hydrabad, de Surat, de Bombay, de Gwalior, et aussi par les lettres interceptés qu'on conte en vous donner une insurrection general en Malwa. Je le crois. Nous sommes preparés. Il faut dire que ne serait pas etonnant si le Nana Sahib pris la parte de tenter sa fortune en sud et d'entrer dans ces pays. Il faut qu'on soit partout sur le qui vive en sujet de ce mechant."

Corroborated at page 67 of Malleson's, Vol. III.

concurring accounts of our own spies represented the insurgents at Mundisore as bent on attacking Neemuch, and one among them, Trooper Thakoor Deen, brought information, as was reported in my letter of 7th September, above referred to, that some of the deserters from our ranks had come in to Neemuch to gather information of our plans, and that the insurgents expected to be joined when they attacked Neemuch by the Native troops in our own camp. That they had reason for their expectation may be inferred from the fact that a Court of Enquiry which had sat on the condition of the Native troops recorded its opinion that the whole ought to be disarmed. Another, and perhaps the most conclusive, authority in corroboration of the view that the Mundisore insurgents contemplated an attack on Neemuch as soon as the road was sufficiently dry for the passage of their guns, is the Nawab of Jowra; copies of his letters of warning under dates the 23rd and 27th August were appended to my report of 7th September before referred to. His last, of the same tenor and more urgent tone, appended to my report of 18th September, I think it right to append here in margin. The testimony I bore in letter of 7th September,

Jowrah, 14th Sept., 1857.

To CAPTAIN SHOWERS,
Neemuch.

MY DEAR SIR,—I beg to lay for your information that the Mundisore rebels intend attacking Neemuch; they will probably march after five or six days, as soon as the roads are a little dry. I have received this information of the rebels' intention from a private source, and I hope you will be on your guard, and send for some more troops, either from Mhow or Nusseerabad, and take every precautionary measures. The rebels are somewhere about ten or eleven thousand strong. I object to your sending in for the Mehidpore Contingent, as I think no reliance can be placed on them.

I hope this friendly communication of mine will reach you in due time and enable you to be on the alert.

I remain, &c.,

(Signed)

GHOUS MAHOMED KHAN,

Nawab of Jowrah.

From COLONEL DURAND,

Offg. Agent, Govr.-Genl.,

Central India.

To THE COMMISSIONER OF DELHI,

Camp Mundisore,

19*th Novr.*, 1857.

(Extract.)

"The Nawab of Jowra has throughout, though surrounded with enemies and difficulties, maintained his loyalty to the British Government."

paragraph 18, to the Nawab's loyalty in keeping me informed of passing events in Malwa, was most satisfactorily supported by Colonel Durand, in the extract from his letter quoted in margin.

That the Nawab's opportunities of obtaining accurate knowledge of the movements and plans of the Mundisore rebels were most favourable, may be inferred equally from the circumstance of his proximity to the place and the fact of a recusant relative of his own, Nawab Abdool Sutar Khan, having joined the movement.

A collision with the rebels was thus inevitable, and the only question that was left for our consideration was, whether to take the initiative, or to await their attack on Neemuch—either alternative, in view of the shaky condition of our Native troops, not without hazard. The decision, however, was precipitated in favour of the former course by the discovery of hostile intrigue at work at Neembahera in communication with the rebels at Mundisore, the details of which were submitted in my despatch before referred to of (7th September). Allusion has been made, in an earlier part of this report, to the suspicions of hostility to the British, attaching to this isolated Mahomedan pergunnah of Tonk from the earliest days of the rebellion. Besides the confirmation now afforded by the intercepted correspondence, certain information had been received that the garrison of Neembahera had been much strengthened of late, and that some of their wall guns had been equipped as field artillery, which of course was not required for merely defensive purposes.

To have awaited an attack from Mundisore on the south, leaving the post of Neembahera within sixteen miles of Neemuch on the north, and commanding the road with our supports at Nusseerabad, in hostile, or even doubtful hands, would probably have entailed the loss of Neemuch and the destruction of the garrison. For this post had been left by Brigadier-General Lawrence without the necessary ammunition for a protracted defence, in disregard of repeated applications on the subject, both by the Commandant, Colonel Jackson, and myself, as brought to notice, and copies appended to my despatch of the 22nd January, 1858, para. 14. No succours could have been sent from Mhow for an indefinite period, owing both to the impassable state of the country in the rains, and to the insurrection making head in Southern Malwa which demanded Colonel Durand's first attention. It seemed essential to our safety, then, to occupy Neembahera, and thus secure at all events our rear, and the line of the only communications left open to us, before the road between Mundisore and Neemuch was passable for the rebels' guns. The steps I adopted to give effect to this resolution were fully detailed in my letter No 188 of the 18th September to Brigadier-General Lawrence's address.

See No. 188 of the 18th September, 1857.

CHAPTER XII.

NEEMBAHERA AND AHWA.

THE Commandant, Colonel Jackson, promptly complied with my requisition to move out a force for the reduction of Neembahera, if it should be found requisite. His entire concurrence in my view of the vital necessity of occupying that place as a stragetic measure, may be gathered from the fact of the difficulties in respect of his Native troops in the face of which he undertook the service. The reliableness of every man in the Native ranks under his command was a matter for the Commandant's calculation. Which to leave behind was as critical a question as which to take. For since but a score of our small detachment of the 83rd (one company in all, reduced by sickness) could be left in charge of the Fort, the chances of a *coup de main* in our absence were to be guarded against. Colonel Jackson's dispositions were most judicious. Having selected such of the Native troops as he considered most trustworthy, the remainder, for the greater part, were detached, previous to the march of the expeditionary force, on out-post duty into the district, a reliable body of Meywar troops being placed at his disposal by myself to strengthen the slender garrison told off for the occupation of the post during our absence.

- 2 9-Pounder Guns.
- 1 8-Inch Mortar.
- 1 Squadron, 2nd Bombay Light Cavalry.
- 70 Rank and File H.M.'s 83rd Regiment.
- 80 Rank and File, 12th Bombay Native Infantry.
- A Volunteer Troop of mounted Gentlemen, 20 strong.

These dispositions being made, a force as per margin marched on the night of the 18th September, on Neembahera. On appearing before the place the following morning, we were joined by a Contingent of Meywar troops, which, in virtue of the general authority delegated to me by the Maharana under his sign-manual, I had directed to rendezvous there. The presence of these in the field, as showing that the Ruler of the surrounding country was heartily on our side, I thought might not be without its effect on such of our native troops as it had been found necessary to take on the service, and tend to steady them. It was for this object principally that the contingent was called out. Requesting Colonel Jackson to halt his force before crossing the stream flowing under Neembahera, I sent a written summons to the Amil by the hand of one of my Chobdars (mace-bearers) to surrender the place to the safe keeping of the British Government till the troubled times should be past, and himself to come out at once to my headquarters in the field in token of submission.

While awaiting the issue of this missive, it may be as well to give a brief sketch of the place before which we had sat down. Neembahera, the capital of the district of that name, is a walled town of just one mile less thirty-three yards in enceinte, the fortifications consisting of nineteen bastions, affording good flanking defences, mean thickness of rampart eight feet of solid stone masonry, of parapet three feet of stonemasonry; wet ditch and berm; height of wall ranging from 12 to 20 feet, according to undulation of ground; four gates, three covered by horn-works of stone, and one by an extensive outwork, defended by outer gates, capable in itself of independent defence. The town contains about one thousand houses, some capable of detached defence, so that the entrance of an enemy might prove but the commencement of his operations for the reduction of the place.

In answer to my summons to surrender the place the headmen appeared, and expressed a readiness to comply. But when it was demanded to give effect to the proffered surrender by disarming the garrison, they feigned inability to control their men. That there never was any real intention to surrender the place, may be inferred from the complete preparations that had been made for defence (their guns even being shotted and replying instantaneously to our first discharge) and from the circumstance of my Chobdar

Vide my despatch to Agent Governor-General, dated 28th September, 1857.

who had been sent in with the summons, being cut down by the Bukshee (chief hereditary official of Neembahera) with the taunt, as the "servant of a Christian," when the gates were slammed to with a shout of defiance. Upon this we commenced operations.

Our guns had been advanced by successive positions to within 150 yards of the East gate, which formed the point of attack, the Infantry skirmishing up under the walls keeping down the enemy's fire from the works, round and chain shot, and musketry. Our attempt to blow open the gate had failed, Corporal Young, 83rd Foot, heading the powder-bag party, having been shot down. No lodgment had been effected nor any impression apparent made upon the place, when, within half-an-hour of sunset, Lieutenant Barnes, Horse Artillery, came up to the position I had taken up at the moment, with Lieutenant Couchman, Artillery, in the Mortar battery, and informed me that the Commandant, being *hors de combat*, a retreat had been ordered on Neemuch. I should under any circumstances have considered it my duty to remonstrate against a step which could not fail to prove more disastrous to British interests in Meywar, on account of the failure of the expedition, than if we had never moved out from Neemuch against Neembahera; but being senior in army rank to Captain Reade, the Officer next in seniority on the spot to the Commander in the field, and who had ordered the retreat, I exerted my military rank, and at once countermanded it. Halting the retiring divisions then, when out of point-blank range, I ordered the troops to bivouac for the night as evening was falling, but before dismissing them I thought it as well to address a few words to the men to remove any possible depression that the order for retreat on Neemuch might have occasioned. The hearty British cheer that rung from the 83rd men on my telling them that the attack would be renewed before daybreak in the morning was an earnest of success.

The enemy fired at intervals throughout the night, but watch fires being prohibited in our camp, no loss was sustained. His last gun was fired about three in the morning.

The gate, against which the attack had been directed during the day, having resisted all our efforts (found afterwards to have been partially bricked up), it was determined to make the attack the following morning at another point. The troops were under arms before daybreak, and the column of assault formed. On moving to the attack the place was found evacuated.

Detachments of the Cavalry were ordered in pursuit of the fugitive garrison. Two parties were overtaken and captured, and among them three of the principal officials. The Bukshee, however, chief permanent official of Neembahera, whose hostility to the British from the earliest days of the disturbances has been already instanced, made good his escape, and fled straight to Mundisore, and joined openly, as a leader, the rebels with whom he had been discovered to be secretly in correspondence.

The British troops were then marched through the town in procession, and the British flag hoisted on the walls with every observance calculated to enhance in the eyes of the Native troops the value of the service they had performed, and the estimation in which it was held by the authorities. This latter object was further promoted by the distribution, subsequently, of a gratuity to the troops, and of special rewards conferred at a public Durbar to those who had most distinguished themselves.

Some of the wall guns in Neembahera were found as had been represented, equipped as field artillery, and fresh gun carriages in hand, half finished.

A solemn act of stern justice, and equally demanded by policy at the juncture, was performed on the occupation of Neembahera. The head putel (chief village authority) of the place was executed at a public parade of the troops by being blown from a gun as reported in my letter No. 286 of 2nd December, 1857, for aiding and abetting gross violence done to my Chobdars, who had been sent into the place, bearing my summons to the Amil, and having done all in his power to compass their destruction, one of them being cut down. The punishment of death, which by the laws of all nations is awarded to the party that respects not the sacred office of a herald, was in this putel's case doubly merited, inasmuch as his own office, as the chief village authority, demanded co-operation in, rather than opposition, to the efforts being made through my messengers to avert hostilities, which if once commenced, must endanger indiscriminately the safety of the peaceful inhabitants of the town.

The effect of the operations generally upon the native troops was most salutary. The apparent confidence shown in taking them on service had reassured them, and although incited to join the rebels by the flag of religion (Deen ka jhunda) being hoisted on the walls before the attack commenced, and themselves called upon to join in the crusade against the British infidels, not a man wavered. On the contrary, the Native troops vied with their European comrades in skirmishing up to within one hundred yards of the walls, and when volunteers for the powder-bag party were called for, many sprang forward. Subsequently the success, its prompt recognition, and the indication generally of our reviving power, fixed their wavering loyalty.

And indeed the service itself was worthy of recognition, considering the handful of men engaged in the reduction of so completely fortified a town, and accomplished with the loss of but 24 casualties, including two European Officers, wounded. The result of the measure may well be admitted as important, seeing that besides the saving of our Native troops, it secured our communications with Nusseerabad, and above all restored British prestige, which, apart from the blow our power had received by the general rebellion (and as yet Delhi even had not been retaken), was suffering at Neemuch from its being supposed that we were cooped up within our entrenchments, awaiting succours. The impression was natural enough,—the outer world being of course in ignorance of the precautionary object, in reference to the condition of our own Native troops, that had suggested the plan of an entrenchment camp under the guns of the Fort. The marching out, however, to the attack of a hostile post, and its occupation, wholly improved the aspect of our affairs. Concurring intelligence from Mundisore informed us that, so far from further talk about attacking Neemuch, the rebels lived in constant apprehension of an attack from us, and from another seriously disturbed quarter, Kherwarra, Captain Brooke, Superintendent Hilly Tract, wrote, that the effect of the measure had been very beneficial in his neighbourhood. At home, within the Station of Neemuch, the changed deportment of the Native troops inspired general confidence. For the first time since the commencement of the mutiny we were absolutely at ease; freed not only from apprehension of attack from without, but also from the not less serious, and infinitely more harassing danger of a recurrence ot attempted risings among our own troops.

With the occupation of the capital, the whole Province of Neembahera fell at once into our possession. In arranging for the Civil Administration, the outline of which was sketched in para. 18 of my despatch of 28th September, 1857, it was my endeavour, as observed, "to let the change of rule in the Province which was necessitated by strategic and political considerations, bring no violent change of circumstance or condition to the people whose lot it had been to pass under many changing yokes." All the district officials who remained at their posts were confirmed in their offices, existing land tenures left undisturbed, local privileges and prejudices respected. From that day to the present,* a period of nearly two years, order in the capital and internal tranquillity throughout the Province of Neembahera, though tried by several irruptions of rebel forces into Meywar, has remained uniformly undisturbed. From this the prosperity and contentment of the people may be inferred.

Greatly, however, as the occupation of Neembahera had improved our position at Neemuch, and in Meywar generally, it was in respect of its retrieving effect, as a counterpoise to the check at Ahwa, of Marwar (which, by a singular coincidence, occurred on the very same day) that the highest and most important advantage was derived. A powerful British column, including European Infantry and Artillery, under the personal command, as well as political guidance, of at once the highest Military

* 19th August, 1859, date of General Report.

and political authority in Rajputana, Brigadier-General Lawrence, being repulsed in an attack on a feudal chief of one of the States, and forced to retire altogether from the field, was at such a crisis sufficiently serious. The disaster was aggravated by the loss of the Political Agent of the district (the chivalrous and lamented Monck Mason), who, having ordered to meet General Lawrence before Ahwa on a fixed day, found on arriving there that the force he expected to find had retreated, when he fell into the hands of the rebels, was killed, his head cut off and placed over the gateway of the fort. A reverse so aggravated was obviously calculated, in the inflammable state of the country arising from the general rebellion, to excite a combination of all the disaffected elements in Rajputana, and thus spread a general conflagration. Powerful elements of such combination existed in abundance in the league of recusant Marwar chiefs on the one side, and of which Ahwa was the head, and in the still more powerful league of the recusant Chiefs of Meywar, on the other side of the border (these last, it must be remembered, having, even in the full tide of our power, displayed such contumacy towards the British Government in the person of the late Political Agent, General Lawrence, as to induce the late Agent Governor-General, Sir Henry Lawrence, to recommend to Government, that the two chiefs at once most prominent in contumacy and most powerful, viz., Saloombra and Bheendur, should be forcibly ejected and deposed from their chiefships by the march into Meywar of two strong British columns). From the closeness of the bond subsisting between the Chiefs in question on both sides of the border, and the promptings of clanship and identity of class interests, the temporary success in rebellion of the Ahwa Thakoor might have emboldened the recusant Meywar Chiefs to take advantage of the general insurrection in India and make common cause with him and his confederates. That they were urgently invited to do so, and with assurances that the aid of the King of Delhie had been solicited, conclusive proof is afforded by the intercepted letters from the Ahwa Chief to Saloombra, despatched immediately on his repulsing General Lawrence's attack. Copy with translations of the same were forwarded to the Agent Governor-General, for submission to the Government in my letter No. 90, dated 25th March, 1858. The originals are in my office. Had the Meywar Chiefs joined the Marwarees, the bulwark that Meywar has presented between the insurrections in Marwar, on the one side, Kotah on the other, and Malwa on the south, would have been removed. The rebel forces uniting, and finding us moreover with wavering Native troops and an ill-furnished magazine, I need hardly point to the consequences of such a state of things.

On the very same day, however, that the check at Ahwa was received, Neembahera was occupied, as above noticed. Considering the attitude of the Meywar Chiefs as illustrated by the reference to Sir Henry Lawrence's plans for their coercion when power was on our side, and the temptations herein afforded by the Ahwa Chief's success, it may reasonably be assumed that they were restrained at this critical juncture, mainly by the sign of reviving power of the British arms in Meywar, as exhibited by the capture of Neembahera.

Vide his letter to my address, No. 193, dated 14th October, 1857.

And yet with respect to this measure of public safety taken at a period of public danger, Brigadier-General Lawrence, my departmental chief, at a distance, objected in the first instance to the proposal, disapproved after the accomplishment, and recommended to Government that Neembahera should be at once restored to Tonk. He would appear (as submitted in my letter No. 188, of 18th September) to have regarded the question exclusively as a local one, and to have overlooked the complications in the contiguous province of Malwa, which, in my central position between two jurisdictions, forced themselves on my attention, and demanded my constant vigilance and frequent active interposition. For the action of the Central India Agency was totally suspended on my borders, consequent on the insurrections in that province. In my Neembahera despatch, dated 28th September, 1857, I had recommended that the measure having been taken partly on strategical considerations, military possession of the walled town should be held, at all events, till the troubled times should be past. That Neembahera has been retained in our hands to the present day,* may be held to afford, practically, a recognition by Government of the weight of the considerations in view of which my responsible action was taken at the juncture in question.

I may here append in margin a letter to my address from the late Brigadier-General Sir Richmond Shakespear, the Resident of Baroda, and commanding Northern Division of the Bombay Army, expressing his opinion at the time of our position in Marwar and Rajputana generally, and the salutary effect of our operations against Neembahera. Sir Richmond coupled his permission, on referring to him about quoting his opinion, with the proviso that it should be added that he was not aware when he conveyed the same to me that my attack at Neembahera

> *Baroda, 28th September*, 1857.
>
> MY DEAR SHOWERS,
>
> Many thanks for your late letters. The Delhi news of the 14th and 15th was very satisfactory. I congratulate you most heartily on your successful affair at Neembahera. It will save the 12th Native Infantry and the 2nd Bombay Cavalry. The Bombay Government will be charmed to hear of it. I sent in the letter at once to Lord Elphinstone's Private Secretary.
>
> But for it, this disastrous business in Marwar (at Ahwa) would have swamped you entirely; but I have great hopes Neembahera (I know the place well) and

* Report dated 19th August, 1859.

Delhi, will carry you on until our reinforcements arrive. The first vessels, which left England in June, have been heard of in Bombay as passing Ceylon, so we may soon expect them.

I think it would be madness for anything short of an army to now advance on Ahwa; but it breaks my heart to think of the ladies at Jodhpoor and Takht Singh, left so long without aid. Alas! for Mason.

General Lawrence, when last heard of, was at Soojat, retiring on Beamar. All Rajputana will be up!

(*Signed*) R. SHAKESPEAR.

had been made contrary to General Lawrence's views. This, however, but adds weight obviously to the involuntary testimony he bore to the soundness of my policy.

Another testimony bearing the imprimatur of official authority may also be cited in support of my policy and its practical tendency to restore British prestige, so seriously shaken in Rajputana at that juncture, viz.: that of the Lieutenant-Governor North West Provinces, Mr. E. A. Reade, the common Superior at the time of General Lawrence and myself. The following are the terms in which he reported to Government the two events at Ahwa and Neembahera :—

Para. 18 of the Lieutenant-Governor's Report.

"The intelligence which has been received from Rajputana is not satisfactory, though of varied character. Colonel Lawrence has had a conflict with the mutineers of the Jodhpoor Legion, now in concert with the rebel Thakoor of Ahwa, without results; and the death of Captain Monck Mason, the Political Agent of Jodhpoor, in an attempt to join him, is a great loss to the public service.

"19. At Neembahera, an outlying portion of Tonk, Captain Showers has succeeded against some insurgents, and obtained possession of their guns."

CHAPTER XIII.

SIEGE AND OPERATIONS BEFORE FORT NEEMUCH.

HAD General Lawrence confined his disapproval of my measure to communicating the same to myself, and submitting to Government such recommendations as he thought fit on the subject, no harm could have accrued. But departing wholly from ordinary official usage, he proclaimed to the Military Authorities at Neemuch, in communications addressed to them, in his capacity at that time of Commander of the troops in Rajputana, his disapproval of my Neembahera policy, a question which in no way concerned them. The tendency of such a proceeding was obviously to affect my position relatively to the Military Authorities, my coadjutors in the preservation of order in Meywar. And hence it came about, as might have been foreseen from such proclaimed official difference with myself by our common official Superior, that both my military and civil coadjutors at Neemuch were encouraged to overlook my authority as unnecessary in their proceedings. So impressed was I with the mischief to the public interests of such a state of things,—of the positive danger that in the still disturbed state of

India might accrue from the want of co-operation between the authorities at Neemuch, that I considered it my duty to bring General Lawrence's proceedings above referred to prominently under the notice of Government, *vide* my letter No. 232, dated 19th October, 1857.

My impressions herein were unfortunately too soon confirmed. Neemuch had enjoyed the repose secured to us by the occupation of Neembahera but little more than a month, when an incident occurred, from which, through the manner in which it was dealt with, the most untoward results ensued.

A body of 400 men had been despatched from Mundisore on the 22nd October, to intercept a convoy of ammunition which was erroneously reported to have left Jowra for Neemuch, and which they expected to fall in with at Kungetee, on the Neemuch road. Being disappointed of their booty they made an unpremeditated raid on the adjoining village of Jeerun, lying within the assigned district under the Superintendency, distant about 10 miles from Neemuch.

The first intelligence of the apprehended approach of this body was sent in by the Thakoor of Kungetee. His letter, addressed to me or to the Superintendent, Captain Lloyd, was opened by the latter. Before sending it on to me, Captain Lloyd endorsed the Thakoor's letter with the following remark under his own signature:—

"It shows that the rebels have not as yet left

Mundisore, nor do I believe that they have any intention of coming in this direction. (Forwarded for the information of the Political Agent, Meywar.)

"(*Signed*) B. P. LLOYD,

"*Superintendent.*"

The opinion here so confidently expressed of the improbability of any approach in the direction of Neemuch by the Mundisore rebels could only be referred, obviously, to the total cessation for some time previously of all rumours of coming attack. Such having been notoriously rife before the occupation of Neembahera, the endorsed remark in question may fairly be held to confirm my view of the sedative effect of that measure.

On authentic intelligence of the descent on Jeerun being received at Neemuch, the Superintendent, without consulting me, though present in the station, took upon himself to call upon the Officer Commanding, Captain Simpson, who had but recently fallen into the command of the station, to march a force to drive the rebels out. They were known to be without guns and ill-provided with small arm ammunition, and the fort at Jeerun to be in a state of dilapidation without any gates. As the plan of attack was matured by the Officer Commanding without seeking any co-operation from me in my official capacity, I inferred that the arrangements made were considered ample for so inconsiderable an enterprise.

A force, as per margin, marched out of Neemuch on the morning of the 23rd October, accompanied in his official capacity by Captain Lloyd, the Superintendent. It returned to cantonments the same night, dejected by failure in the object of the expedition, the rebels being left in possession of Jeerun, to complete the plunder of the place. The depressing effect of this retrograde movement was enhanced by the number of casualties sustained. Out of eleven officers present on the occasion, two were killed* and five wounded. The heads of the two officers killed were cut off by the enemy, and Tucker's carried away and placed over the gates at Mundisore, attended by the gross and unmentionable outrage by which, among certain savages of India, scorn as well as hatred for their fallen enemies is expressed. This trophy, for as such it was looked upon by the enemy, to confirm the too true vaunt that a party of 400 undisciplined rabble, without a single trained soldier in their ranks, without guns and but indifferently armed, had repulsed in open fight an equal number of our British troops, with artillery, was eminently calculated to encourage hopes of success on the

H. M.'s 83rd.
3 Officers.
50 Rank and File.
2nd Light Cavalry.
2 Officers.
255 Rank and File.
12th Native Infantry.
2 Officers.
100 Rank and File.
2 9-pounder guns.
1 Mortar.

* Captain Reade, 83rd, and Captain Tucker, 2nd Light Cavalry.

part of the rebel leaders at Mundisore in an attack on Neemuch while under such military command.

So strongly impressed was I with the serious character of the Jeerun reverse, as calculated to bring about an attack on Neemuch, that I sent intelligence of the event the morning after its occurrence to Colonel Durand, at Mhow, as well as reporting it to Brigadier-General Lawrence, communicating my view of the probable consequences. I ventured to urge upon General Lawrence the adoption of precautionary measures in view of the attack that might now be anticipated. But General Lawrence accepted another version of the situation; and treated my apprehension as without sufficient foundation. A supply of ammunition even, which had been urged on his attention by the officer late in command, Colonel Jackson, and myself, some months previously, was still delayed. The correspondence on this essential point has already been fully submitted to Government in my despatch No. 20 under date 22nd January, 1858. Colonel Durand, on the other hand, most fortunately for the safety of the post and the garrison, had a truer apprehension of the event reported, and of our changed position at Neemuch in consequence. His reply is appended in the margin. Concurring with me, it will be

Extract from Colonel Durand's dated Camp Dhar, 29th October, 1857.

"I am sorry to learn by

yours of the 24th, that your Neemuch troops had a reverse at Jeerun. This may embolden the Mundisore rebels to move against Neemuch before we are ready to advance thither."

observed, in believing that the result of the Jeerun affair might induce an attack on Neemuch, he expressed his intention to march on Mundisore in progress as soon as the work cut out for the Mhow Column in his immediate vicinity was over.

Captain Lloyd, the Superintendent, who had called for and accompanied the expedition, reported the result of the Jeerun affair to Brigadier-General Lawrence as a "victory," basing his representation upon the circumstance of the rebels having subsequently evacuated the place. The fact was that having been left in possession by the reverse and retreat of the British force from before the village to plunder it at leisure, they returned the following day to Mundisore to carry back their spoil and the trophies which the incident of the fight above noted had placed in their possession.

But for my rightly apprehending, and faithfully representing, the nature and probable consequences

"I know well the state of affairs at Mundisore and have as earnest applications from the Chiefs and Scindias authorities as from yourself, the same from Saugor which is probably beset. Ditto from Hoosungabad and Bhopal directions."

of the Jeerun reverse, Colonel Durand might have moved with the Mhow Column in another direction (and other calls, as will be seen by the appended extract from the same letter, were urgent), instead of marching towards Neemuch. How opportune, how vital, was his diversion, will appear in the sequel.

The effect produced by the Jeerun check changed the whole aspect of affairs at Neemuch. It was but two days afterwards that the Superintendent conveyed to me the rumour of a threatening inroad in force into the district (vide para. 2, my letter No. 255, of 29th October, to Agent Governor-General), and similar rumours prevailed almost daily from that date in the station, causing the bazaar to be deserted in panic, till, culminating in an authentic report of the march of a body from Mundisore, they appeared before Neemuch on the 8th November, *i.e.* about a fortnight after the Jeerun affair.

On approach of the enemy, the regular Cavalry (about 250 sabres) was ordered out to meet him. The officer in executive command, as he designated himself (Captain Bannister), called upon me before mounting, in company with the Superintendent (Captain Lloyd), to seek my co-operation with my body-guard of Meywar troops. I joined him with 300 Horse. We met the enemy advancing across the downs beyond the nullah forming the rear defence of Cantonments. On our approach he formed line in open single files so as to display as extended in front as possible, and showed many flaunting flags. His numbers appeared about 2,000, of which 100 were horse; of the foot, between 500 and 600 were fighting men (vilayatees) but undisciplined, the remainder armed rabble who had come, probably, in the hope of plunder. On forming up, the enemy opened fire from three guns. I proposed to Captain Bannister a combined charge on the enemy's position. This movement was strongly urged by Colonel Jackson, who was in the field without command, having retired. Captain Bannister declined on the ground of restrictive orders from the officer in command of the station, but who, being on the sick list, was unable to take the field. After observing the enemy for about an hour, he retired altogether from the field, retreating upon the fort. The rebels then breaking again into column of route continued their march towards Neemuch. Observing this, I advanced the Meywar detachment in the direction of the bridge over the nullah so as to oppose a check to the enemy's entry. The movement had the desired effect. The enemy halted, brought his guns to the front, and opened fire again; and thus he stood held in check till nightfall, when he bivouacked on the same spot. The Meywar detachment was then withdrawn from the field, a strong picket being left at the bridge. Among the officers the only casualty was Lieutenant Stapleton's horse shot under him. In my despatch of the day's operations (see Appendix), I commented on the mischievous anomaly of an officer in the field acting under general restrictive orders from a commandant not in the field.

On reconnoitring the enemy's position at midnight, and finding him still bivouacked on the ground where he had received the check, I proceeded to the fort and communicating the circumstance to the Officer Commanding, strongly urged his moving out the troops to attack the rebels at daybreak. I left him to confer on the plan, as he proposed doing, with the Artillery Officers. At daybreak he came to my house to say that it had been decided not to attack the rebels, but to occupy the fort with Infantry,—the Cavalry to keep the field.

It only remained for me then to keep the field also with the Meywar Horse, in order that, by joining forces, the combined Cavalry might be in a position to operate effectively against the rebels, and thus best aid the garrison which had taken to the fort and was prepared to be invested.

About an hour after sunrise, the rebels, finding no preparations made for attacking nor even to resist them, streamed unopposed and unobstructed into the station, and with ringing yells of triumph fired every house that was left standing amidst the ruins of the former conflagration of June, when the Neemuch brigade rose in revolt.

The Officer Commanding the regular cavalry in the field marched straight away from Neemuch, in disregard of my official remonstrance against his doing so, in quest, as alleged, of his baggage and spare horses, and never came again within sight of the fort till the siege was raised. I remained in observation with the Meywar Horse alone, preventing the enemy's horse from over-running the country, rescuing several parties that had fallen into their hands, and communicating daily with the garrison, as reported in my despatch to Brigadier-General Lawrence's address dated Neembahera, 11th November, and copy of which was forwarded direct to Mr. Secretary Edmonstone in my letter to his address of the same date. The practical advantage derived by the troops in the field from the possession of Neembahera in our hands at that critical juncture was adverted to in those despatches. See Appendix for extract copy of last para. of my transmitting letter to Mr. Secretary Edmonstone.

The temporary success of the rebel force in having been suffered to march unopposed into Neemuch and sit down before the fort, was daily attracting supporters, both horse and foot, to the Shahzada's standard before the walls, and producing a disastrous effect throughout the surrounding district of the British superintendency. Several of the chief towns, on receiving the Shahzada's call to allegiance, ejected the British authorities and declared for him. Jawud, Ruttengurh, Singolee, all rose in open rebellion. On the other hand, the disappearance of the regular Cavalry from the scene of operations was producing not unnaturally a dispiriting effect upon the Meywar Raj irregulars in the field with me. On the 3rd morning of the siege (the 11th) I was advancing with but a handful towards the fort from Kasoonda, a village within sight of Neemuch where I had encamped during the night, when a single troop of the regular Cavalry (about 60 sabres) hove in sight. The officer in Command, Lieut. Farquharson, stated that he had been detached by the Officer Commanding the 2nd Cavalry to proceed and co-operate with me. My remonstrance had effected thus much at least.

Thus reinforced, I had no hesitation in turning my demonstration of the preceding day into a real attack on the rebels' position before Fort Neemuch. Advancing from the south, we swept rapidly down upon the villages of Bugana and Nixongunge, their Head Quarters. Taken completely by surprise, our advance being concealed partially by high standing jowarree crops, the rebels fled in a panic. Many were cut up,—some burnt alive in huts that were fired. These villages and the nullah in rear of the fort being completely cleared, we were enabled to communicate personally with the garrison to arrange for a sortie in co-operation. The Cavalry meanwhile were to remain halted on the other side of the nullah till the sortie party should be ready. Then the Cavalry, making a demonstration on the enemy's rear to the south to draw their force off to that side, would have left the way open for the sortie party to dash out and spike the rebels' only siege gun, which annoyed the garrison. This plan was unfortunately frustrated by some misconception on the part of the Officer commanding the troop of 2nd Cavalry, for it appeared in view to the north of the entrenchments, a movement calculated to draw the enemy in that direction instead of to the south as the proposed demonstration would have done. And so it happened: for on joining the troop we saw the enemy's horsemen, issuing at first stealthily by twos and threes—for they had not yet recovered the panic caused by our first dash upon their position—begin by degrees to stream out from the rear of the Infantry Hospitals and to gather in a group on the easternmost side of the Brigade parade ground, on which the Cavalry troop was now formed up. When they had increased to about 50 in number, I urged the Lieutenant commanding the troop to charge them. But instead of doing so he went "threes left" and inclined away, the men firing with their carbines. All this time the enemy were increasing rapidly till they amounted to about equal in strength with the troop, and, emboldened by our not charging them, they began to advance towards us. It was apparent then that a charge was the only thing that could avert a disaster. So, exercising my military rank, I gave the word "Halt, front.—Charge!" placing myself at their head, with Jackson, who was in the field as an amateur. Instinctively at the word they halted and formed line—probably the troop horses obeyed the accustomed word of command of their own accord—but instead of following in a charge the troop broke into column again. Thereupon Colonel Jackson, solicitous for the honour of his regiment, the 2nd Cavalry, as well as keenly alive to the critical condition of the moment, called out, "For God's sake, charge. Gentlemen, you will lose your names and disgrace the regiment." The troop continued moving to the flank, nevertheless, firing their carbines. The enemy, who had been advancing at a walk, emboldened by this hesitation, now broke into a gallop. Then, to use the words of Colonel Jackson in letters dated the 17th December, 1857, addressed to Colonel Green, the Adjutant-General of the Bombay Army, and Captain Macgregor, of his own regiment, describing the scene—then "the head of the column bolted away at speed, the centre followed, and the troop became totally disorganized in flight." The next moment the enemy was upon us. Jackson and myself, a Parsee clerk of my office, the brave young Anderjee, and a mounted chuprassie, Gopal Singh, were only saved by being splendidly mounted—the two latter on my own horses, as usual when attending me in the field. Cutting our way through towards a wide nullah (ditch) formed by percolation through the embankment of the tank to the north of the parade ground, we pounded our pursuers by clearing it, and gaining the top of the embankment circled round it at speed. A shout of mingled rage and disappointment followed us, with a parting random volley. Jackson here well remarks, in his letter to Macgregor: "Had it not been for a stiff nullah, several of us would have bit the dust." My two mounted Meywaree orderlies were both killed. Gopal, my chuprassie, had his thumb cut off in defending a rifle which he was carrying in his hand. Retiring upon Neembahera, we encamped securely under its walls.

The affair of the morning having been witnessed from the walls of the Fort, an express from Lloyd, dated 5 p.m. of the same day (11th), writing in cypher that they were running short of ammunition for the guns and of sheep for the garrison, adds: "We are anxious to know how you and Colonel Jackson fared this morning."

Keeping up communications with the garrison was daily becoming more and more precarious. The last letter received was from the Officer Commanding, written in cypher and concealed in a quill, mentioning that they were running short of small arm ammunition. Having gathered from some of our men who had escaped from the rebel camp during the confusion and panic occasioned by our Cavalry operation, that the enemy were preparing ladders for escalading the Fort, I communicated this intelligence to the garrison, suggesting their not throwing away a shot, as reported in my despatch of the 11th November above referred to. An attempt at escalade was made a few days afterwards, and successfully repulsed by the fire of the garrison without any of the rebels' ladder party getting within 50 yards of the walls, or any loss sustained by the garrison. How far the intelligence I had communicated of the enemy's plans and the precautions I had suggested thereupon may have contributed to this result I am not aware. As the information itself was obtained as one of the fruits of our Cavalry attack on the 11th, the operation in question, equally in view of the important enterprise contemplated, and the early partial success of the attempt, may perhaps be held as not unworthy of recognition. The first partial success of that operation, though executed with but comparatively a handful of men (not above 80 sabres in all), may lead us to infer what conclusive results, in the contemplated raising of the siege, might have attended the attack if the whole of the Regular Cavalry had been co-operating at the time, especially as in such case the garrison might have been emboldened to make a sortie at the same time.

Fort Neemuch had now been besieged for two weeks, and was still closely invested by the rebels, whose numbers had greatly increased by the unexpected advantage they had obtained in getting possession of the Cantonment unoppcsed. The ammunition of the beleaguered force was running low, and there appeared no prospect of any supply being thrown in—a convoy, indeed, was forwarded by General Lawrence from Nusseerabad, but too late, the Officer in charge, Captain Baumgartner, having been recalled while en route on receipt of intelligence of the close investment of the Fort by so large a body of the insurgents. On hearing of its despatch I wrote to Captain Baumgartner* mentioning the arrangements which I had made for strengthening his convoy on its approach to Nee-

* Vide copy in Appendix.

much, but he had already retired in obedience to his recal to Nusseerabad. The surrounding district under the British Superintendency, having almost wholly declared openly for the rebel Shahzada, no supplies of any kind could be thrown in. Internal tranquillity in Meywar fortunately remained undisturbed. Still, since no effective relief could be afforded by the States, in consequence of the rapid growth of the movement and increase in numbers of the investing rebel force, the situation of the garrison had become most critical.

At this juncture, Colonel Durand appeared on the scene. Acting on his expressed view, above given in concurrence with mine, which was conveyed to him immediately on the occurrence of the Jeerun affair, that it might bring on an attack on Neemuch, he had marched with the Mhow column in relief, and now threatened Mundisore. The siege of Neemuch was at once raised (on the 22nd November,) the investing rebels returning by order of the Shahzada to defend Mundisore. Neemuch and its little garrison were thus saved, but I think it may be fairly assumed that, but for my timely report to Colonel Durand and his right apprehension of the true state of the case, both might have been sacrificed by General Lawrence's withdrawal of all official confidence and support from me, at a moment when our interests in Meywar were in so critical a position, and by his accepting the version of the Jeerun affair as reported by Capt. Lloyd in preference to mine, whereby Neemuch was left short of ammunition for a sustained defence. The entire destruction of the rebel force by the Mhow column on the 23rd, and flight of the Shahzada and other leaders of the movement, left Neemuch secure. The Kotah rebellion, it is true, was at its height, but I had long since had the ghat leading from Harowtee into Meywar broken up so as to be impassable for Artillery at all events.

Two incidents of the siege of Neemuch seemed to me, in view of the loss of prestige, and the consequent disastrous effects in the surrounding country arising from the same, to call for public enquiry.

First, that a band of undisciplined rabble should have been suffered to enter and burn the Station, and shut the garrison up in the Fort, without their being attacked by the British Troops, although the circumstance of their having been brought to a check by a small body of Meywar Troops, as undisciplined as themselves, and thus held in check a whole night, afforded at once an opportunity to the Officer Commanding, of reconsidering his decision, and an assurance doubly assured of conclusive success, if any such indeed were needed in the case of undisciplined rabble being attacked on an open plain by British Troops, greatly superior in two arms, Artillery and Cavalry, and not so inferior, numerically, but that the proportion of European Infantry in our ranks must have altogether counterbalanced the disproportion in numbers. And second, the Officer Commanding the Regular Cavalry marching away from the vicinity of the beleaguered fort, notwithstanding my strong official remonstrance, instead of remaining to co-operate for the relief of the garrison. Impressed with a sense of the expediency of an enquiry being instituted into the conduct of the two Officers severally responsible for these acts, I submitted my views to that effect in a letter No. 279, dated 25th November, 1857, detailing the several points for enquiry. None was instituted, however, as Brigadier-General Lawrence had approved of the proceedings of both Officers, both in not moving out to attack the enemy on their appearing before Neemuch,* as any reverse would in all probability have involved the loss of the fortified square and destruction of all the force, and again in the second instance noted, in the Officer Commanding the Cavalry not risking an encounter with the enemy.

* Vide his letter in acknowledgment, No. 202, dated 12th November, 1857, copy appended in Appendix.

As embodying a different view on the point in question, I would here cite the recorded opinion on the above detailed operations, of an Officer of rank, and of acknowledged military repute, who was present throughout—Colonel Forbes Jackson, late commanding at Neemuch, in letters to Colonel Green, Adjutant-General of the Bombay Army, and to Captain Macgregor, a brother Officer of the 2nd Bombay Cavalry, dated 17th December, 1857.

"The advance of the rebels on Neemuch on the 8th November was a complete surprise. About 2 o'clock, p.m., information was brought that a party of them had occupied a village about five miles from Neemuch, and almost before the Cavalry could move out to meet them, they arrived and formed on the parade ground across the bridge on the south of the Bazaar. I reconnoitred them and they did not appear to me to be more than 800 men drawn up in single line in open files, with their baggage cattle in rear so as to deceive us as to their numbers. A more brilliant opportunity for a glorious success and victory could not have offered. They were evidently afraid of their own audacity, for they never attempted to advance one pace from their position towards Cantonments, even after the 2nd Cavalry had disappeared out of sight, and only the Meywarees occupying the bridge. Why the guns were not sent out in support of the Cavalry was, and is, an enigma to me. Without crossing the bridge the guns might have poured shrapnell and case into the enemy. Even supposing they had crossed and were compelled eventually to retire on the fort, you know the road is open and free of all obstacles to interrupt a retreat at full gallop. During the night I reconnoitred them again, I found them precisely in their first position. They entered Cantonments in the morning, totally unopposed."

On the military question raised by the above-stated contrary views of the two authorities cited, viz.: whether the rebels' attack on the station of Neemuch on the 8th November, 1857, should have been opposed by the garrison, or supinely submitted to, I would leave my military readers to form a judgment, and feel assured that it hardly needs to recur to the Napoleonic maxim in war to point the lesson taught by this incident of the hitherto unwritten history of the period.

Before closing this chapter relating to the irruption of the Mundisore Shahzada's force into the Neemuch district, let me pay a passing tribute of affectionate regret to the memory of my faithful servant, Ooserie, who sealed his fidelity with his life. When patrolling daily with the Meywar Horse around the invested fort, I used, on leaving my encampment in the morning, to send Ooserie on a riding camel with my despatch-box and a change of clothes straight to whichever village I purposed encamping at at night. One fatal day, in making his short cut, some of the rebel horsemen came upon him, unattended by any escort, captured and took him in to their leader who held his head-quarters in the old Residency, built by Sir David Ochterlony. They charged him with remaining in the service of the Chief Civil Officer. They questioned him as to the contents of the despatch box, supposing it to contain valuable jewels. He could only reply that it was his master's office box. Disbelieving him, they tried to wrench it open. Resisting their efforts, some one suggested that it might be an infernal machine to explode on being forced open, and purposely thrown in their way to destroy the Shahzada. The box was at once flung out of the open doorway, and the faithful and true Ooserie, innocent of all crime but fidelity to his master, was taken out and killed. There was a shocking story reported as to the manner of his death, but I refuse to believe it. The thought of a faithful servant losing his life for pure fidelity is distressing enough without being harrowed by the reflection that he was tortured. The despatch-box was found unopened in the Residency compound after the siege was raised. It bears the marks of the wrenching iron to this day.

CHAPTER XIV.

FINAL OPERATIONS AGAINST TANTIA TOPEE.

THE dispersion of the Mundisore movement and consequent return of security at Neemuch seeming to render my continued presence there no longer necessary, I proceeded to Oodeypore, and remained at the capital till July of the following year (1858), when the incursion of another rebel force, under Tantia Topee and Rao Sahib, into Meywar, after Sir Hugh Rose (the late Lord Strathnairn) had driven them out of Gwalior, necessitated my return to Neemuch to confer with the Officer Commanding on measures for attacking them.

In the interval the first detachment of the reinforcements from England detailed for Rajputana had arrived on the 12th April, when a wing of the 72nd (Seaforth) Highlanders marched into Oodeypore in progress to Neemuch, under Captain Crombie. This was the first Highland regiment that had ever come to India—the first of "the Blue Bonnets come over the Border." The natives were equally astonished as delighted at the splendid physique of the men and the striking and picturesque plumed bonnets and tartan plaids of their uniform; but above all were their hearts stirred in sympathy with the martial bag-pipes so near in unison with their own wild war-skirls. "It is the most exquisite music," the Minister remarked as the piper was playing in ascending the winding stairs of the palace at a fête given to the regiment by the Maharana; "it is the most exquisite music we ever heard—it is enough to charm a snake out of its hole." And the piper played before the King, who presented him with a handsome honorarium. The three days the Highlanders halted at the capital were devoted to sport and festivities. There was shooting in the surrounding hills for the sportsmen; the lake was alive with pleasure boats and state barges, on which the other officers and men embarked to visit the lake islands with their water palaces, now become historic as the place of refuge of the Neemuch refugees. In the evening the officers honoured me with their company at dinner at the Residency, wound up by a Natch held under a Shamiâna or curtained canopy spread over the terrace. The scene had at least the charm of novelty to my friends, as the first of the Arabian Nights entertainments that awaited them in the glowing East.

Tantia Topee and Rao Sahib, entered Meywar at the head of a force of about 5,000 men, composed partly of the British revolted native soldiery. On intelligence being received that they had passed Mundelgurh, and were approaching the Ruttungurh-Singolee passes, through which a passage would have been opened to the Chumbul, at Rampoora, and thus a retreat out of Meywar, Brigadier Parke, who was in Command at the time, moved out a field detachment at my suggestion to take up a position above the Jawud Steppe, so as to command the south exit of the passes in question. The required position was attained by a creditable military operation, under the immediate command of Major Taylor, 2nd Bombay Cavalry, the detachment, with its artillery, being taken up the Sookdeo ghat—never before crossed by an organized force. The object of this move was completely attained. The rebel army was held in check. The tract of country lying between the Chumbul and Bunas rivers, comprising some of the most fertile districts of the British Superintendency, as well as the territories of our ally, the Maharana of Oodeypore, was for the greater part saved, and the inhabitants, who had fled to the jungles in dread of the impending irruption, were enabled to return to their homes.

The rebel force, headed back by the advance of the Neemuch Detachment, crossed the Bunas river, and was thus thrown upon General Roberts' force then advancing into Meywar, and which met and defeated Tantia at Sanganeer on the 9th August.

The object of the move of the Neemuch Field Detachment above the steppe having been thus accomplished, it was withdrawn, and Tantia having retreated westward after his defeat at Sanganeer, Brigadier Parke moved a force under his personal command westward at once to cover Oodeypore and command the passes leading south into the Banswarra jungles. This move also had the desired effect. Supporting the advance to the Capital of a detachment of Native Troops which had been moved up on the requisition of my Assistant at Kherwarra, Captain Annesley, the move of the rebels on Oodeypore was checked, and the passes into the Banswarra jungles being occupied, and the passes westward into Marwar closed by my direction, Tantia was again thrown upon General Roberts' force which had followed upon the tracks of the retreating rebel force after the affair at Sanganeer. The action of Kotaria ensued on the 14th August, where Tantia lost four guns and retreated eastward again, re-crossing the plains of Meywar.

Brigadier Parke then took up the pursuit, and accomplished the first of that brilliant series of operations by flying columns, which has marked the campaigning of the second year of the rebellion in India with its distinctive character, operations which for celerity of movement, endurance of extraordinary privations and fatigue, and practical tranquillising results, stand unsurpassed in the annals of warfare, and in the conduct of which Brigadier Parke's name as a Commander stands prominent. On the occasion in question, after following awhile in hot pursuit on the track of the rebels, it soon became evident that they were making for the fords of the Chumbul, at Rampoora, by a hill route that our guns could not traverse. Sweeping along the base of the Jawud Steppe, then, the force arrived on the 20th at Neemuch, within thirty miles of the Chumbul, having attained this advanced position to cut off the rebels' retreat, by a succession of forced marches over a country deep with the saturated soil of the monsoon, and through an August sun. A fresh detachment was at once pushed on half-way to the river as an advanced guard, and thus matters stood on the 20th. The intelligence received from Holkar's authorities at Rampoora of rebels' movements was submitted to the Officer Commanding, and the fate of Tantia and his force seemed decided. The *contretemps* by which the rebels nevertheless escaped across the Chumbul, passing the ford but six hours before the arrival there of the Neemuch force, on account of the delay occasioned by the conflicting intelligence of Tantia's movements communicated to Brigadier Parke was reported in my letter No. 234, under date 24th August.

About four months afterwards, that is, in December, Tantia Topee and his rebel force made a second irruption into Meywar, the events connected with which were fully detailed in my Report No. 369, under date the 26th December, 1858, and may be here briefly sketched.

After his defeat at Chota Oodeypore, on the Nurbudda, on 3rd December, by Brigadier Parke, who had been in hot pursuit of the rebel force ever since the last irruption, but partly beyond the limits of my jurisdiction, Tantia Topee re-entered the Meywar territory from the south, near Koosulgurh, of Banswarra. A gallant attempt was made by the Rao of that place, one of the Frontier Chiefs, to oppose his entry, for which he received an honorary reward from Government; but the rebel force was too strong to be successfully resisted by the Banswarra Native Levies. Carrying all before him, then, Tantia occupied the Capital of Banswarra on the 11th. The Maha Rawul's palace, however, had not been carried when the opportune arrival of a British detachment under Major Learmouth, 17th Lancers, saved the town from being sacked, Tantia proceeding northward on its approach towards Saloombra.

The threatening attitude assumed by the Chief of Saloombra, in concert with Bheendur, on the strength of the rebel force being encamped at his capital, was duly reported in my despatch above referred to. The demand which I received at that juncture, when alone and unsupported at Oodeypore, for the immediate redress of their alleged grievances, conveyed in letters to my address from the Saloombra and Bheendur Chiefs and received together by the hand of one and the same messenger, came invested with a peculiarly sinister significance in view of the presence of the rebels at Saloombra, and of certain information that an advance on the Capital was contemplated. My summary dismissal of the messenger with a verbal admonition and pregnant warning, as further reported in the same despatch, at once foiled their attempt at intimidation, and had the effect of restraining these contumacious Chiefs from irretrievably committing themselves to the cause of rebellion.

Tantia, with his whole force, marched from Saloombra on Oodeypore, but unaccompanied and unsupported, openly at all events, by the Chief, Rawut Kesree Singh or by members or retainers of his faction. All practicable preparation for the defence of the capital was made. Still, in view of the threatening attitude of the banded recusant Chiefs and the uncertainty how far their intrigues might have been at work among his own foreign troops within the walls, the Maharana was anxious. At his Highness' request, then, the Neemuch Field force was summoned by express to cover the Capital.

The demonstration was sufficient to divert Tantia's march on Oodeypore. Turning off at Geengla, he moved north-east on Bheendur.

The Capital being thus secured, I moved out and joined the advancing Field Detachment under Major Rocke, and directed its efforts exclusively to holding the rebel force in check from breaking northward out of the Jungle Tract, in order that Brigadier Parke, who was advancing from the south, might come up with it again. To that end, successive positions were taken up which served, as reported at the time, to head rebels back at two points where they attempted to break (thereby saving incidentally the Chiefship Capitals of Konore and Bara Sadree), and finally to drive them back south.

The detachment which had been posted in observation of the Pertabgurh passes on east of the "Jungle Tract" (the literal meaning of Banswarra), having been withdrawn at that juncture to form part of a force required to watch the fresh irruption of rebels under Feroz Shah into Central India, Pertabgurh was left uncovered. As this capital lay in the direction in which Tantia had retreated and was especially obnoxious to attack equally as a rich city for plunder, and in reprisal for the life of a former leader of the rebels, Kasim Khan Vilayutee, whom the Rajah attacked and killed on his entering the Pertabgurh territory with his followers, after the defeat of the Mundisore rebel force in November, 1857, Major Rocke's detachment was moved by a forced flank march to cover Pertabgurh. It arrived there on the 23rd December. A glance at the map showing the low jungle tract surrounded by the elevated plateau upon which Major Rocke's column was operating, will, as exhibiting the extent of the outer circle, give an idea of the rapidity of the movements demanded to hold Tantia from breaking cover from his vantage point at the centre of the circle, and to attain the required position in question on the date named, the 23rd. And, as it proved, none too soon—for on the following morning I received intelligence that Tantia, with his whole force, then about 5000 strong, and accompanied by some 4000 Bheels under the Bheel Chiefs, who had given him refuge in their jungles, and had shown him the Pertabgurh Pass on a promise of sharing the plunder of that rich State Capital, was in full march upon it. Major Rocke's column, of the force noted in margin, being too weak to detach guards for the protection of the camp while marching out to meet the approaching rebel force and to cover the city, the camp was struck and sent into the city with all camp equipage—baggage, cattle, &c.—for security within its walls. The column then marched westward towards the Banswarra Ghât to cover the city. Intelligence arriving that the head of the rebel column had already debouched on the Pertabgurh plateau, the column took up a defensive position on a rising knoll on the westernmost extremity of the city wall. The distance from the Ghât being but about three miles, the enemy soon loomed into view in dense masses, and, taking up a position surrounding us on three sides at a distance of about two or three hundred yards, opened a musketry fire. Our infantry replied, and our guns fired shrapnell and grape. While this fusilade action was in progress, the rebel cavalry formed up on our left flank with apparent intention of charging. The mutinied 5th Bengal Irregular Cavalry being conspicuous in this movement, and keeping its formation as if on parade, I looked on with mingled pride and regret. Having

1 Squadron, 2nd Cavalry.
2 9-pounder guns.
2 Companies, 72nd Highlanders.

formerly been adjutant of the regiment, I could hardly suppress a secret feeling of gratification at observing the good drill they exhibited, while to see a once faithful corps of gallant soldiers led away by the designing to believe the artfully concocted stories of our designs on their religion, was indeed lamentable. But this was not the time in the midst of a sharp conflict against great odds to indulge in moralising—so, trailing our two guns "*action left*," a few rounds of grape served to repel the intended charge. No further attempt to assault our position was made. At night-fall the enemy's fire slackened, then ceased; and it soon became apparent that favoured by the darkness they had retreated round both sides of the city to the eastward in the direction of Mundisore. Pertabgurh was thus saved. I immediately sent information of Tantia's repulse and retreat to Captain Hutchinson, who, with the 17th Lancers, was watching another pass out of the jungle tract about 12 miles further to the south. Colonel Benson then took up the pursuit, thus saving Mundisore; and subsequently he overtook Tantia at Zirapoor and routed him with slaughter.

In our action at Pertabgurh considerable loss was inflicted on the enemy, including a leader of note, as indicated by the appointments of the corpse and the circumstance of the usual device in such cases having been adopted by cutting off the head and carrying it away to preclude identification. There was nothing on the appointments of the richly accoutred body to afford a clue. Many prisoners, elephants, &c., fell into our hands. The troops, on that cold Christmas Eve, bivouacked on the field.*

The defeated remnants of the rebel force, reinforced after their second expulsion from Meywar by Feroze Shah and his followers some 2000 (two thousand), swept round through Upper and Western Rajputana, pursued and attacked by several columns in succession at different places, and entered Meywar for the third time from Marwar on the

* It is necessary to expose here the undeniable errors into which Colonel Malleson has fallen in his account of the events above related. The marginal catchword at page 357, "Baffles Major Rocke," is his version of the energetic and successful efforts made by Rocke's slender column, first in saving Oodeypore from the threatened attack, next heading Tantia back when attempting to break cover at two points, Konore and Bara Sadree respectively—thereby incidentally saving these two chiefship capitals from pillage—and finally circling round and getting into position to cover Pertabgurh in time to meet Tantia advancing upon it, and defending this capital from the concerted pillage which had been Tantia's bribe to the Bheel Chiefs for shelter in their jungles. This fact further refutes that author's statement that "the Bheels, far from aiding Tantia, followed his track as the vulture follows the wounded hare, anxious for the moment when she shall lie down and succumb." That Tantia himself could not conceive it was the same force which had checked his advance on Oodeypore that opposed him at Pertabgurh, is evident from his deposition which is appended to Malleson's Vol. III. Therein, after alluding to the "tidings of a British force, which made him retrace his steps to Bheelwarra," he speaks of having "fought at Pertabgurh with a body of English troops which had come from Neemuch."

west in February, 1859, or about two months after their previous irruption. Brigadier Somerset's Column being at the time in the field in Meywar in observation of the Ghat, I proceeded at once to join him. Missing the rebel force by a few hours at Lake Kankrolie on the 17th, the efficiency of this admirably equipped brigade, the most powerful and complete in its appointments of all the flying columns organized by General Michel, was fully tested in the following pursuit, and in the successful result of the operation rewarded at once the care that had been bestowed in its equipment and the energy of the Commander. Though the rebel force had nearly a day's start, and had fled south-east, its retreat to the Banswarra jungles was cut off. Forced then to keep the open, it soon became disorganized by the unflagging, unrelenting pursuit. After the second day stragglers began to fall into our hands at every mile. One leader, Nawab Abdool Suttar Khan, broke off with his followers from the main body while in mid-flight, and soon afterwards surrendered. Another leader, Feroze Shah, sent in a deputation to me with overtures for terms, and which resulted in the immediate surrender of his principal officer, Peer Zuhoor Alli, with 300 (three hundred) followers, as reported in my despatch No. 48, dated 1st March, 1859, General Michel joining Brigadier Somerset's camp to receive the surrender in due form.

CHAPTER XV.

EXECUTION OF TANTIA TOPEE.

THE last sparks of the rebellion were now stamped out. Tantia Topee saw that the game was up. Indeed he had long seen it, and had wished to retire from the field. Of this fact we have the testimony of his formal deposition taken on the 10th April, 1859, and authenticated by the Commander of the Field Force, by a detachment of which Tantia's seizure had been effected on the 7th idem, while a solitary fugitive in the Parone jungles, to which he had retired after carrying out his purpose of quitting the field. The words of the deposition must be here quoted to form a judgment regarding his claim to mercy, in withdrawing from the war while his master, the Rao Sahib, was still, at the head of six thousand men, prepared to continue it. "I had been quarrelling with the Rao Sahib all the way from Deogurh Bâri, and told him I could flee no longer, and that whenever I saw an opportunity of doing so, I should leave him. The opportunity for doing so here offered, and I left him, and accompanied the three above-named parties in this

(Parone) direction. When I left the Rao Sahib, he had about six thousand men with him. But three men, two pandits to cook my food, and one saes (groom) and three horses and one tattoo accompanied me. . . . We reached the Parone jungle and met Rajah Màn Singh."

The story of the way in which Man Singh was worked upon by his natural desire to recover his lost patrimony to betray his trusting friend into British hands, is not pleasant reading for an Englishman. Though aware that he had surrendered to the British, Tantia did not distrust his old comrade for a moment, but sent for him to consult him; the presumption hence being that in pursuance of his virtual surrender in quitting the field, he contemplated the formal act, following the example of his friend. Man Singh went, but accompanied by a party of Sepoys held in ambush. Finding Tantia asleep, they seized and carried him into the British camp. He was then marched to an obscure outstation, Sipree, and tried before a court-martial on the charge of having been in rebellion, and having waged war against the British Government between June, 1857, and December, 1858, in certain specified instances. No charge of having murdered, or having been privy to the murder of any British subject was alleged against him; and he emphatically denied having been guilty of any such act.

Had he been allowed counsel to defend him, it might have been urged on his behalf: 1. That he was no subject of the British government, his opposition to which could be rightly construed into criminal rebellion against his sworn allegiance; on the contrary, that he was the servant of a foreign master, the Nana Sahib, the son of the Peshwa Bajee Rao, the liege lord of all the Mahrattas, whose orders he was bound to obey. 2. That his master's political wrongs in being disinherited from the provision solemnly guaranteed by the Company's Government to his father had enlisted such sympathy, notwithstanding the revulsion which all must have felt at his personal crimes, as had served to shield him against the bribe of a lack of rupees, (£10,000) offered by the Government for his person, alive or dead. To this day the Nana's fate remains absolutely unknown. Equally so that of his successor, and Tantia's second master, the Rao Sahib. 3. That such breach of faith, as they regarded it, had forced his master to be a conspirator, and that he himself, and his compeers, had only done their duty in taking up arms at his bidding. Again it might have been urged on his behalf that the spirit of the Royal Amnesty protected his life: "Our clemency will be extended to all offenders, save and except those who have been or shall be convicted of having directly taken part in the murder of British subjects." No such charge was ever alleged against Tantia. Nevertheless he was sentenced to be hanged—and was hanged. History will ask, who approved and confirmed that sentence?

Contrast Tantia's case with that of Dewan Mool Raj of Mooltan, charged with the murder of Agnew and Anderson. He was allowed a fair trial at Lahore, the capital of the province in which his alleged crime was committed. And an experienced British officer was appointed to aid him in his defence. Strong were the presumptions against the Dewan. He had been superseded in the governorship of Mooltan by an order of the Lahore Durbar, the Punjab being then—the year 1848—under the Protectorate of the British during the minority of Maharajah Duleep Singh. Agnew and Anderson, both Assistants to the Resident, were sent down to relieve Moolraj and take charge of the district. They were well received by the Dewan, who bowed in well-feigned submission to the order of the Durbar, virtually that of the British Resident, Sir H. Lawrence. Agnew, it appears, called for a formal statement of account, which, with equal apparent submission, was professed should be duly rendered. The two officers then left the fort where the interview had taken place, and, mounting their horses, rode homewards towards the house in the suburbs appointed for their residence. On the way an angry crowd gathered around them, and being unattended by any British escort, they were attacked, and one of them wounded. Setting spurs to their horses they distanced the mob, and reached their residence. But the mob followed them. Streaming through the undefended gateway it filled the compound, and with angry shouts called for the "Feringhees." The last scene was described by one of our officer's servants on his return to Lahore. The two Sahibs were in an upper room of the house, one tending his wounded comrade, when multitudinous steps were heard on the staircase. Feeling, from the determinedly hostile attitude of their assailants, that in their utterly helpless condition their last hour was come, they shook hands, bidding each other an eternal farewell. The pattering footfalls have gained the landing: the next instant the armed throng crushes in through the narrow doorway into the room, and the two Englishmen, confronted by overwhelming numbers, calmly await death with the hereditary courage of their race. Their heads were cut off and carried away, whether as voucher for the deed done, or to set up, as is too often done, in derision, did not come out on the trial. The presumption of instigating to the deed was strong against the Dewan, but positive proof was wanting, and being, as above observed, ably defended by a skilful advocate, Colonel Hamilton, Commissioner in the Punjab, his life was saved.

Contrast his case again with that of Tantia. Consider that the last sparks of the rebellion had been completely stamped out, that no emergency existed for an example to strike terror, and reviewing the circumstances of his execution at the period in question by the light of the contrast afforded by the action of the Government on previous similar occasions, history will, I fear, only too justly pronounce, that it was a pitiful proceeding, quite unworthy of British precedents. Regarded, again, by the light of the Royal Proclamation, seeing that no charge of the murder of any British subject was ever made against Tantia, and that in his defence he voluntarily declared his innocence of any such act, the future verdict, it is to be apprehended, will be that it would have been more generous, more just, more in accordance with the spirit of the Queen's gracious Amnesty and Act of Oblivion, to have commissioned Man Singh to arrange the formal surrender of the broken-spirited and virtually surrendered refugee, than to betray his trusting friend, doomed by a foregone conclusion, to an ignominious death.

CHAPTER XVI.

THE QUEEN'S PROCLAMATION.

ON the assumption by the Queen-Empress of direct rule over India at the latter end of the year 1858, it fell to my duty, as Resident in the Meywar States, to promulgate the Royal Proclamation at the Military and Civil Head Quarters of my circle—Neemuch and Oodeypore respectively. Before describing the ceremonial observed on each august occasion, it may be advisable to refer to the events which created the necessity for the measure—and this the more particularly because the latest writer on the subject, Colonel Malleson, evinces in the opinion he has pronounced on the point,*—that the change arose from the necessity of finding a scape-goat for all the blood which had been shed—a total misapprehension in regard to the responsibility for the policy which brought about the Mutiny. He has rightly followed Kaye—without acknowledgment however—in ascribing that event to the annexation policy of Lord Dalhousie; but, in endeavouring to absolve the East India Company from all part and participation in that policy, he shows

* History of the Indian Mutiny, Vol. III., pp. 357-8-9.

that he has not studied the history of the first measure of the series, the annexation of Satara, upon which the battle of the policies was fought. The question was raised by Lord Dalhousie, on the death of the late Rajah in 1848 without any lineal descendant, whether it would, or would not, conduce to the consolidation of the Indian Empire to absorb the Native States upon every "legitimate" opportunity—to get all India within a "ring-fence," according to the cant phrase of the annexation school. To facilitate an answer in the affirmative of the proposition, it was suggested that a denial of the right to adopt heirs, on failure of lineal descendants, would sooner or later prove an effective axe to lay at the root of each dynastic tree. That the original conception of the policy was Lord Dalhousie's, we have the testimony of his Minute of 30th August, 1848. Since a ready reference to this Minute may be convenient to collate with the late Governor-General's other papers, which, by the directions of his will, are to be published fifty years after his death, I think it as well to attach a copy of the Minute in question in the Appendix, to be referred to at that juncture.

In thus plausibly applying the rules of succession obtaining in European States to the feudal principalities of India, the rational origin of the practice of succession by adoption, obtaining among the Native States, was overlooked—to guard, viz: against anarchy through the possible extinction of a dynasty in a single battle-field, by the death of the reigning prince, with all his sons fighting and falling around him. Again, the necessity of a successor to perform the funeral obsequies of the departed is essential to Hindoo salvation, not to speak of the rights and interests of the subordinate Chiefs and people, preferring their own native rule to the British. Now in regard to the responsibility for the decision arrived at on the issue in question—*re* Satara, the Court of Directors approved of and upheld Lord Dalhousie's views by an overwhelming majority. Mr. Ross D. Mangles wrote a minute of approval, which was subscribed to by nine of the Members of the Court. There were four able dissentients who recorded their minutes of dissent—Colonel Oliphant, Hon. Leslie Melville, H. St. George Tucker—the fourth, I am ashamed to say, I forget at the moment, and have not the means of reference in the country where I write. Without the powerful and overwhelming support of the Court of Directors Lord Dalhousie would have been utterly powerless to carry such a momentous innovation in principle of Indian policy, the more especially since the highest local authority, Sir George Clerk, the Governor of Bombay, within whose jurisdiction Satara lay, was wholly opposed to it, as was also the lamented Bartle Frere, Resident of Satara, acting under him. The public now may judge with what justice, knowledge, or appreciation of the dignity of history, Colonel Malleson describes the solemn national act by which the Queen and Parliament of this great Kingdom accepted the high responsibility of the rule of two hundred millions of subjects as a mere shuffle of the cards called for by the necessity of finding a scapegoat in the innocent Court of Directors, similarly as "if India had been at that time under the rule of the Crown, the natural scapegoat would have been the Ministry of the day?" No: the change of rule after the Mutiny was absolutely imperative. Directly responsible as the Court of Directors were for the Annexation Policy, recording their approval of the original conception on principle, and officially approving and confirming each successive act of annexation, the noble words of the Queen's Proclamation: "We shall respect the rights, dignity, and honour of native princes as Our own," would, in the mouth of the Court of Directors, have been a barefaced mockery. Uttered by the Queen on reversing the policy in question, the words were a message of reassurance and of peace which, together with the Royal Amnesty, literally, to use the trite metaphor, were as "oil upon the troubled waters."

The further government of India by the East India Company had become impossible. The hour and the man had come! The "India of the Queen" was henceforth the only possible Government!

In raising my voice against the Court of Directors of the East India Company in respect of the point here at issue, I would not be misunderstood. My loyal devotion to my grand old Masters was inherited from my ancestors of three generations—their military servants, whose services date back to the early foundations of the Indian Empire. It was confirmed by my own experience of their generous protection, from the first gift of my appointment by the lamented Mr. Neill Benjamin Edmonstone down throughout the long series of favourable recognition of my humble efforts by my departmental chief and honoured friend, the late lamented John Stuart Mill, and others. It is not without a searching of heart then that I have steeled myself to pen a word to their apparent disparagement. But Historic Truth is sacred. "If it be not Truth," as Kaye well observes in the preface to his "History of the Sepoy War,"—"if it be not Truth, it is not History."

On the 11th November, 1858, the troops at Neemuch were drawn up on the grand parade for the celebration of the inauguration of the Queen-Empress' assumption of direct rule in and over India. The troops being formed in hollow square, I rode on the ground accompanied by the Rao of Bedla and the Oodeypore Minister, with their brilliant *cortèges*. These, the highest noble of his State, and his Prime Minister, the Maharana had deputed to assist at the ceremony in token of his satisfaction at the auspicious change of rule, then inaugurated. The pregnant significance of such a public act on such an occasion on the part of the highest Hindoo Prince in India, and the recognised head of the great Hindoo Confederacy, under the ancient title of "Hindoo-Put," can hardly be over-estimated. The Royal salute by the guns on parade which succeeded my reading of the Proclamation was re-echoed by the distant booming of the guns of Fort Neembahera. A *feu de joie* followed. And as the band was pealing forth our National Anthem, the assembled troops broke forth into an involuntary "Three cheers for the Queen!" in which the gallant 72nd, Seaforth Highlanders, were conspicuous by waving their bonnets high aloft on the points of their bayonets.

In the evening a public dinner was given by the Highlanders, followed by one to the European troops. Joining them after mess, accompanied by the officers, I had the honour of addressing the men and proposing the Queen's health, which was drunk with renewed cheers. Illuminations and fire-works closed the first day's rejoicings.

On the second day (the 12th) there was a public banquet given by the Maharana at the Oodeypore Minister's residence, to which, by His Highness's desire, I had invited all the garrison. The Rao of Bedla, on behalf of the Maharana, proposed the Queen's health; the Commandant, Major Rocke, responding, proposed the Maharana's. In returning thanks for His Highness, I expressed my conviction that the assurance conveyed in the Queen's Procla-mation would enhance the gratification which the Maharana and all the Princes of India would feel in being brought into nearer relation with her Majesty.

The following day (14th) illuminations in the town

of Neemuch, promoted by the able Superintendent of Jawud-Neemuch, Capt. Dennys.

The following day (15th) a public dinner by the Parsee community in honour of the occasion, accompanied by a brilliant illumination. After the Queen's health, I proposed that of the Parsee Community of India, coupling the name of Sir Jamsetjee Jeejeebhoy with the toast—improving the occasion to pay a well merited tribute to the distinguished personal qualities of the race, and to that loyal recognition of the protection they had enjoyed under British rule, which, in the recent period of danger, had led them to share that danger as if of one and the same nation.

20th November. To Jawad, by Dennys' invitation, to assist at the fêtes proposed to be held at the district Capital, in honour of the occasion. Although the inhabitants had shewn disaffection when the Shahzada attacked Neemuch, I conceived that in assisting, nevertheless, at this demonstration of loyalty, I should but be moving in the spirit of the Act of Oblivion promulgated by the Queen's Proclamation—letting by-gones be by-gones. Illuminations general.

Proceeding, then, to the Capital, I had again the honour of reading the Proclamation at a Grand Durbar, to which all the feudal chiefs, high and low, had been specially summoned by the Maharana. A royal salute was fired; the streets and palaces, and lake islands, were lit up at night with illuminations of a brilliancy and character which, viewed afloat, owed its striking effects to the city approach to the lake lying through a Venetian Canal, spanned by its own picturesque bridge, with its own old-world legends clustering about its arches. The steps of the temples, and palaces, and bathing ghâts on either side were thronged with a sea of heads of holiday makers in gay attire, cheering with loyal acclamations as, seated in a state barge with his Highness and his brilliant suite, we were rowed slowly down towards the lake. The temples clanged forth their "harmony of discords" from pealing bells and brazen horns. The several *nobut-khanas*, or native bands, rang forth their shrill clarion notes in succession as we passed, but above all thundered the din of the sham-fight fireworks, representing in the cross-fire maintained over our heads between the buildings on either side, with the flashing of coloured lights and deafening reports, a battle of the Titans—

> "Warring in Heaven, 'gainst Heaven's matchless king."

Disembarking at the palace stairs, we proceeded, mounted on elephants, through the illuminated streets of the city before returning to the palace to dinner.

As a fitting sequel to these public manifestations of satisfaction at the Queen's assumption of the direct Government of India, Maharana Soroop Singh addressed a letter of congratulation to Her Majesty. Translated, in the following words:—

(AFTER DUTIFUL RESPECTS AND COMPLIMENTS)

"The announcement made in the Royal Word, that the Queen of England is coming to rule over us, has shed light and joy over this darkened land like the moon rising upon the night. Impelled by the emotions which fill my breast, I hasten to offer my humble tribute of loyalty to your Majesty, and with the involuntary outpouring of my joy, I desire to mingle the expression of my grateful sense of the solicitude for your Indian subjects, evinced by the act by which your Majesty has taken us all under your immediate protection, and thus removing the late intermediate link, has riveted the chain of affection by which my humble throne is brought nearer, and bound inseparably to your high throne.

"The gratification at this proof of your regard for our welfare, which all the princes of India will, I believe, share equally with myself, is enhanced by the assurance so graciously given by your Royal word that your Majesty will respect the rights, dignity, honour, and religion of Indian Princes as your own. Not that this assurance was needed for my own satisfaction, for I had ever confidence in the magnanimity of England's Queen, who, as the Ruler of so mighty a nation, could afford to indulge the promptings of her generous heart towards her protected princes.

"I desire to offer my congratulations on the crushing of the head of the great rebellion, which has swept like a vengeful Avatar over this land. I had no doubt myself of the end that has been accomplished so entirely in accordance with my hopes and prayers. It was equally a gratification to me, as it seemed a duty, to reassure in that dark hour of danger, many of my brother sovereigns who, when cut off from the accustomed support of British troops, applied to me for counsel, and reminding them of the benefits we had all experienced under British protection, to advise all to stand firm with me in our loyalty to your Majesty's throne and Royal person. All of these have shown their fidelity accordingly by standing steadfast through all difficulties. But to few was it given what fell to my good fortune, to be enabled to show my unalterable attachment to the British Rule, by extending my humble aid and protection to the British refugees, when betrayed by the revolted soldiery cantoned within my territories.

"That the auspicious change in the Government now inaugurated may prove to India, still smouldering from the recent conflagration, like rain from Heaven, at once quenching the fire and enovatinn the soil; that the consciousness of the benefits your Majesty will have extended to millions by that act may increase the happiness of your own heart, and, reflected, create an additional source of gladness and guardian interest throughout your Royal Family—is the earnest hope and prayer of your Majesty's faithful and most devoted servant." *(The Oodeypore Royal Seal affixed.)*

This letter, in Khareeta, or royal form, enclosed in the usual cloth-of-gold and cambric envelopes, was forwarded in a golden casket, lined sandal wood, representing in its elevation and plan, a model of the water palace, Jug Mundir. This I had designed at the Maharana's instance, as the most appropriate token to commemorate the incident referred to in his letter, in regard to the repose and protection found by the British refugees within its island home. The elephants' heads, on which the casket rests, rise in the original structure out of the water, conveying the idea of the palace floating on the surface of the lake, supported by swimming elephants.

If, amidst the thunder of cannon and tumultuous rejoicings incident to this august occasion, the faint tremulous throbbing of an individual pulse may without intrusion find audible expression, I might perhaps be pardoned in adverting to the personal gratification which I could not but feel, and pointing to the poetic justice, at being made the official mouthpiece of proclaiming so prominently the reversal of the policy against which my humble voice had been consistently raised from the earliest day of its sinister inauguration; but the fallacy of which had only been demonstrated by the logic of a Mutiny demanding the shedding of oceans of blood for its suppression.

CHAPTER XVII.

WHITHER?

AFTER describing "The India of the Queen" under its varied aspects of 'Expansion,' 'Consolidation,' 'Conciliation,' and "The New Leaven," the writer of the brilliant articles recently published in *The Times* concludes his able review of the subject with a consideration of the tendency of the changes indicated under the heading of the momentous question—"Whither?" I purpose in the present chapter to consider the same question by the lights afforded by the writer, illustrated or modified by those of my own personal lifetime's experience of India, and the lessons especially of the troubled period which I have endeavoured in the preceding pages faithfully to describe. The *Times* correspondent discriminates with just observation the total reversal of the conditions of the problem of government with which the East India Company had to deal from those now presented to the Queen's Government. With the former, it was to divide and govern; with the latter it is to unite and rule. The remark that, "when the Company allowed its problem to get the mastery, it fell—the Mutiny being the direct result of uniting the Princes and Sepoys in a common animosity and fear before the Government had the appliances for rendering the force of the Empire rapidly available at every point"—was precisely foreshadowed in the concluding words of the Author's memorandum on the Annexation Policy previously referred to as having been left on record at the India office in the spring of 1856. "Such a policy to be carried out with safety," it was observed, "would demand the presence in India of 100,000 extra bayonets. Would it pay to hold India on such terms? The only answer which any practical statesman could return would be: *Quieta non movere.* Let well alone."*

* The memorandum in question being a Paper placed on record at an early date, and the views embodied in it having been so exactly verified by subsequent events, it would have been satisfactory to the Author and doubtless to the reader, if it could have been appended *in extenso* in this place. But the copy which he took out on returning to India in the autumn of 1856 (the same one submitted to Lord Canning through his private secretary, Mr. Talbot), Sir Henry Lawrence had taken with him to Lucknow "to read at leisure," so he said on asking for it, after glancing at the commencement. After the siege the Author wrote to Sir Henry's nephew, Mr. George Lawrence, who was his private secretary at Lucknow, and was referred by him to his father, who was one of the executors. He was subsequently referred to Sir Herbert Edwardes, who was writing the life of Sir H. Lawrence. Edwardes wrote in reply that he had not come across such a paper. He concluded then that it had been destroyed in the fatal chamber where the shell burst that deprived India and his country of one of the best and noblest of men. Recurring then to the original left with the Under-Secretary, Mr. Henry Danby Seymour, the Author applied to him on return to England in 1860. He kindly made every search for it, but wrote to him finally on the 7th August announcing a fruitless search. His letter is now before him along with the others relating to the lost memorandum.

The difficulties of governing an united India, indicated by the *Times* writer, are mainly three: 1, Over-population; 2, The status and armies of the Feudatory States; and 3, The aspirations for a share in the government of the country on the part of the natives of India. These difficulties, he adds, are of our own making. In respect of the first, the writer remarks: "The result of civilized rule in India has been to produce a strain on the food-producing powers of the country such as it had never before to bear." It has become a truism of Indian statistics that the removal of the old cruel checks on population in an Asiatic country is by no means an unmixed blessing to an Asiatic people. The restrictions which war, pestilence, and famine formerly presented to an increase of the population have been counteracted by our measures. "That increase," the writer considers, "has of late years expressed itself in large and appalling figures." His apprehensions herein I cannot share. In marching over the country I have often ridden for miles over an obviously fertile soil, as indicated by its surface growth, but totally uninhabited—hundreds of thousands of acres of land only awaiting the plough. The writer proceeds: "The obvious remedy of emigration has meanwhile been tried and failed." I am constrained to join issue as to the obviousness of this remedy, believing that "migration," not "emigration," is the true solution of the problem in India as in Ireland. I had the honour of expressing my views to this effect in the public papers during the discussions on the Land Act in 1881, advocating the adoption of the "Reclamation" clause in deprecation of the "Emigration" clause, and that the Reclamation works should be effected as Imperial works. Similarly in India. Many of the artificially formed lakes and other works of material beneficence left as monuments of their enlightened rule by some of the former rulers of India, might serve as models for us now. My lamented friend, the late Colonel Dixon, followed their lead in the Mhairwarra district under his charge and transformed, by the construction of over one hundred lakelets, a wilderness into a garden, and reclaimed and settled down on the lands so recovered, the immemorially wild lawless Mhairs. It was a party of these men whom, on the outbreak of the Mutiny at Nusseerabad, he sent down, by a dying inspiration, to seize and occupy the arsenal at Ajmere. No: the problem of excessive population need have no terrors to a government that knows how to deal with its available resources, and recognising in every able-bodied subject a potential element in the wealth of the nation, has the honesty to apply that knowledge impartially, without respect to the selfish influence of interested classes. Indeed, the correspondent, reviewing the new appliances, railway and other, at the Government's disposal, does not wholly despair. "The battle of civilization against over-population" (he concludes this head of his subject), "has not yet been lost, and it may yet be won." For "may" let me read "shall."

The second difficulty indicated by the *Times* writer has reference to the status and armies of the Feudatory States. He approaches this subject with a due conception of its importance. A mistake here nearly lost us India, by the token of "these tears," and might, as the sagacious writer sees and says, again "imperil British rule." While advocating a "new departure" in our dealings with the Feudatory States as, in his opinion, inevitable, in view of the new military exigencies of the Government, consequent on the Indian frontier having become almost conterminous with the armed camp of Europe, he is at a loss how to formulate the terms of his "new departure." Impressed with what he conceives to be the "growing loyalty of the Indian Princes," as illustrated by the Nizam's recent offer of money to aid in our frontier defensive arrangements, the correspondent would trust the Princes, but is staggered by one great historical fact which he conceives stares us in the face, viz., that "the main function of the armies of British India has hitherto been to keep watch and ward over the Native States." Let me reassure him by citing a departmental incident within my knowledge, showing that the Native States under good hands need no troops to keep watch and ward over them—an incident so strikingly exemplifying the sound practical statesmanship which marked the career of my first honoured chief in Rajputana, the late lamented Colonel John Sutherland, that it deserves to be exhumed from the pigeon-holes of the Foreign Office and publicly recorded at once in his honour and in that of the Native Princes to whom he was accredited. On the annihilation of the Cabul army in 1842, and the urgent call for troops that then arose, Colonel Sutherland, among other Political Officers, was called upon to state what troops he could spare from his circle. Rajputana at that time was garrisoned by 15,000 men. He answered, "All." The whole were accordingly withdrawn. Order and public tranquillity remained absolutely undisturbed within the extensive and varied region of the Rajput States. Lord Ellenborough, the Governor-General of that day, on Sutherland's application for sick leave in consequence of a sunstroke received when we were boar-hunting at Ulwar, remarked, "The loss of that one man may make the difference of 15,000 men to the Government." Durand, who was Private Secretary at the time, mentioned the incident to me.

The above exhibition of loyalty, although passive, at a crisis of unexampled public excitement, was followed a few years afterwards, in 1847, still under Colonel Sutherland's auspices, by a striking proof of active loyal effort on the part of the Rajput States on behalf of our Government in sending their troops into the field for the operations against the marauder movement organized by the outlawed chief, Thakoor Jowahir Singh—a revival of the redoubtable "Duke Werner" of Italy in the fourteenth century, at the head of his "Great Company." The formidable character of the movement was shown by the exploits of the band, first in the forcible rescue of one of their imprisoned comrades from the central jail of Agra, and next, in the attack and successful plunder of the Government Treasury at Nusseerabad—both stations being military garrisons. A force was ordered to take the field to punish the outrage on our authority and to put down the movement; but the contemplated employment of regulars was overruled by Sutherland in favour of operations by the troops of the Native States exclusively, placed under my command as his military *attaché*. These operations, owing mainly to the hearty co-operation of the States, were entirely successful, resulting in the capture of the outlawed Chief with his principal followers after a harassing pursuit, under my immediate command, into the heart of the great Western desert and assault on his stronghold. Thus quiet was restored to the country and the authority of Government vindicated without the necessity of a desert campaign, costly as it must have been at any rate, and the issue in the circumstances obviously doubtful. Lord Hardinge, who was Private Secretary at the time to his father, the late lamented Viceroy, may be able to speak as to the estimation in which the service in question was held by

Government. I could go on multiplying instances, but need perhaps cite no more than that of the Maharana of Oodeypore detailed in the preceding pages, to reassure the *Times* correspondent against the imaginary danger of a policy of trust in our dealings with the Feudatory States.

In alluding to the troops of the Native States being disciplined by us at their expense, the correspondent leaves it doubtful whether he contemplates the forces so disciplined being permanently officered by British officers. If so, that would but be inaugurating the system which it was contemplated in the year 1879 to introduce. In exposition of the impolicy of that system I addressed *The Times* from India on the 20th March, 1879. *The Times* did me the honour to publish my letter in its issue of 16th April. I endeavoured to show that it would be but an extension on an enormous scale of the subsidiary system which had been tried in India on a small scale, and at every critical juncture had failed, as it deserved to fail, being virtually a fraud on the States. Their money is taken from them to raise and equip and discipline a force by European officers who, left in command, the paying Prince is reduced to a cypher. He not only has not the services of the force he pays for, but being located for the most part in the territory of the Prince, it overshadows his independent position. But in the strain of the Mutiny the Nemesis came. All the contingents in Bengal mutinied to a man, and most of them killed their officers. The Gwalior contingent, numbering some 8,000 strong, distributed throughout some four or five stations, the Kotah contingent, the Mehidpoor contingent, the Jodhpoor legion, the Bhopal contingent, &c., all mutinied. Now, if it be asked what inherent defect is there in the subsidiary system that as a rule renders it so unreliable in point of fidelity to the commanders of its legions, I answer, the fact of the knowledge of the men that they are eating the salt of one party while commanded by another. Fidelity to his salt is the highest honour of man in all stages of society. In the lower grades among the natives of India the feeling is intensified by the terrors of superstition. "*Namuk haram!*" (faithless to thy salt) is the last reproach among Orientals. It would be dangerous, then, I think, to entertain the belief expressed by the correspondent, and practically rely upon it in any crucial case, that this deep-rooted feeling engrained in the lowest depths of native Indian nature, and the paramount promptings of self-preservation, under the law of Political Gravitation, can ever be adequately superseded by an abstract sentiment of loyalty to the throne.

The *Times* correspondent proceeds: "This question of confidence lies at the root of our whole position in India. How far is it yet safe to trust the Princes? how far is it yet safe to trust the people?" I have endeavoured to furnish an answer to the first part of this question by citing the action of the head of my office at critical conjunctures. I may also point to the facts related in the preceding pages, as affording further corroborative response. We have seen that the Maharana of Oodeypore, who had been denounced by my predecessor, was trusted by me to the last extremity of consigning the British refugees, including many women and children, to his guardian care. How well he justified that confidence was shown by his protection of them, and forwarding them eventually under his own guards to distant British posts in safety. Again, by the counsel he gave to his brother inferior princes seeking his guidance as their traditional head when struck with panic at the revolt of our Native army, to stand steadfast to the British, following his own example. Again, in several minor instances which have been detailed in the preceding pages, and finally by his open demonstration of satisfaction at the inauguration of the Queen's direct rule in India. While trusting the Princes, then, and they responding to our confidence in the manner exhibited, you may trust their retainers who under the feudal institution are but a reflex of the head of the state. It is not here as in the independent jirgahs of the north-west border tribes, where every man fights for his own hand. My last word about the Native States is solemnly—let them alone! If you attempt to manipulate them with whatever good intentions, they will crumble under your hands like mummies, and then you would be confronted with the responsibility of having to govern trackless wastes and jungles, deserts for hundreds of thousands of square miles, yielding little or no revenue, with the fierce light of European civilization beating on your administrative system—the speedy result being hopeless bankruptcy. It was my cherished privilege during the earlier years of my training under Colonel Sutherland to read letters to him from his old official chiefs, Mountstuart Elphinstone and Metcalfe. One from the latter in this connexion immediately occurs to me. Writing on the annexation of Sindh, he observed: "What a fatality attends us in India—we cannot touch without destroying!"

I think I cannot better conclude my remarks on this head than by quoting the last sentence of my letter to *The Times* above referred to—a letter, the arguments and historic examples adduced in which, supported by the imprimatur of *The Times* columns, served to stop the scheme for the conversion of the native armies then on the *tapis*. And that it may still do such good office at any emergency of doctrinaire meddling in the future I will append it to this little book that it may be available for ready reference. "Let us, then, only so order our rule in India in relation to the Native States that since all history exhibits them as owning nominal allegiance to some suzerain, they shall feel that the just and tolerant Protectorate of the British is the best possible condition under which they could subsist, when, as in the great Akbar's time (300 years ago), and in our own of yesterday, so in the future, the brave retainers of our loyal Feudatories will ever be found ready to defend our cause, and, as identified with it, their own."

The *Times* correspondent's third difficulty propounded has reference to the aspirations for a share in the government of the country on the part of the natives of India, and how far it is yet safe to trust the people? This political problem is complicated in his view by the religious movement described in his fourth article under the head of "The New Leaven." He recognises its working in "the deadening of the old fanaticisms, the dismemberment of the old superstitions, the death of the old beliefs." But this result was only what was to be expected from the high class and exclusively secular education provided by the Government universities established in 1857 and their affiliated institutions. The correspondent observes that "Many Indian thinkers, Hindoo, Mahomedan, and missionary, look forward with apprehension to the effects of a national education which is destructive of the national faith." I do not share their apprehensions, but am disposed to hail it as a good omen, in concurrence with the view expressed by *The Westminster Review* so far back as 1865, when, in an article on "The Principles of our Indian Policy," the writer, in reference to the dying out of the old faiths that might be anticipated, thus expressed his hopeful view of the result: "In the highest matters of religious faith, especially in a heathen land, the belief in the old faith with all its degrading superstitions has to die out before the mind can be fit to receive the impressions of the true. The 'Centre of Indifference' is the transition state through which the Pilgrim in his Progress must pass from the 'Everlasting No' to the 'Everlasting Yea.'" In proceeding, then, to the consideration of their political aspirations, we need have no fear that in the pursuit of them the natives of India will be led by infidelity into the excesses of the populace in the French Revolution, setting up a ribald "Goddess of Reason" as the Supreme Arbiter of the world. If there is one moral quality which pre-eminently distinguishes the natives of India, I should be disposed to name it, the attribute of Reverence. An almost superstitious regard for antiquity—for immemorial usage under the common phrase, "*Bap dada ka chal*" (the customs of their fathers and grandfathers), is engrained in their nature. In abandoning, then, their old beliefs in stocks and stones, and all the supernatural powers vested by superstition in these idols, under the conviction forced upon them by secular education as to their utter inadequacy to fitly represent supreme power in the moral governance of the world, they do not deny that governance. The Bhagwan of the Hindoo—the Allah of the Mahomedan—have ever represented respectively to these differing creeds a supreme controller of the world. That belief, under whatever form it may be manifested in the seething fermentation of the "New Leaven," will operate as a restraining influence in their pursuit of political power, upon which the Government of India may confidently count.

The Queen's proclamation promised the people of India a share in the government of their country. The Government has deliberately educated them to fulfil that high destiny. The Queen's government of India, as the *Times* correspondent well observes, "has preferred the dangers of popular education to the perils of popular ignorance." And rightly so. The preposterous belief in the greased cartridge would be impossible at the present day. It was absolutely heart-breaking to witness the crass credulity of that fatal period. Not even the superstitious fidelity to their salt, nor the memory of a century's indulgent protection, nor the devoted confidence of their regimental officers who had led them in a hundred fights, and still trusted them to the death, weighed for a moment against the supposed design on their religion. Well, that day is past—never to return. The danger of the future, if danger it be, will assume another form. Here we are confronted with the correspondent's question: "How far is it yet safe to trust the people?"

I think I cannot better open the discussion which this pregnant question challenges, than by citing the commencement of a minute of Mountstuart Elphinstone, the concluding words of which, as the emanation in my humble judgment of the highest political wisdom, I shall certainly quote in peroration. On a plan for the establishment of an institution for the Education of the Revenue Officers, and for the formation of a Native Civil Service, submitted to him when Governor of Bombay in 1824, by Captain John Sutherland, afterwards my first official chief in Rajputana, as previously referred to, Elphinstone recorded the following minute:—

> "It would be a narrow view of the plan proposed, to regard it as terminating in the supply of a better description of revenue officers. The effects are far more extensive, and the benefits to which it may ead are of a much higher order. Among the most prominent, are the facility which it would give for the safe admission of the natives into a larger share than they now possess of the administration of the government; and the means which it would put into our hands of influencing the conduct of the whole population, and of diffusing throughout it the knowledge and sentiments which we are most desirous to impart."

To those who have witnessed the results of Elphinstone's wise and enlightened rule in India, in the growth of the institutions he founded, and the good feeling of the people, conciliated by his large-hearted sympathy in their welfare, the mention of his name would be sufficient authority; but to that not inconsiderable class who, from want of opportunities of forming a personal judgment, are constrained to take public men in India according to the official recognition of their merits, it may serve to recommend Elphinstone's opinions to their approval when I add that, besides being Governor of the Bombay Presidency, he was, after return

N

home, twice importuned, at critical conjunctures, to go out as Governor-General,—his general acceptance as an authority need not further be insisted on. Let us hear, then, what he has to say regarding the state of public feeling towards India on the occasion of the direct rule assumed by the Queen in supercession of that of the East India Company. Referring to the discussions in Parliament, he wrote, on the 30th April, 1858, to Sir Edward Colebrooke: "It is most astonishing, considering how much our safety depends on the contentment of our Indian dependents, that in all the late discussions there has not been a single speaker of note, except Gladstone, that has laid the least stress on this part of the subject."

Having adduced this high testimony to Mr. Gladstone's statesmanlike interest in India, evinced and publicly advocated thirty years ago, I will only further quote his latest words on the same subject, uttered in March, 1885:—

"I hold that the capital agent in determining finally the question whether our power in India is or is not to continue, will be the will of the two hundred and forty millions of people who inhabit India, their positive or negative will, their anxiety, or at least their willingness, to be in connection with us rather than encounter the mischiefs or the risks of change. The question who shall have the supreme rule in India is by the laws of right an Indian question; and these laws of right are from day to day growing to laws of fact. Our title to be there depends on a first condition that our being there is profitable to the Indian nations; and on a second condition, that we can make them see and understand it to be profitable. It is the moral, and not the military questions which stand first in the order of ideas, with reference to the power of England in India as much as with reference to the power in England itself, of the State over the people."

This view of the benefit of the people of India being the first condition of our continuing in India, the second being that we can make them see and understand it to be profitable, runs on all fours with Elphinstone's. It derives singular significance in respect of its reaction on our home Government from the fact observed by the *Times* correspondent that within the period of the Queen's reign the altered relations of India to Great Britain have totally changed the whole scope and purpose of our foreign policy. In the early part of the reign the foreign policy of England was a policy of European responsibilities, as those responsibilities had been bequeathed to us by the gigantic struggle with Napoleon. To-day our interests are Asiatic, our European policy in great part depending upon our need of a safe high road to India for ourselves, and a strong frontier for India against possible invaders. The centre of interest in our mutual relations having been shifted to India, our internal policy for India must be shaped in conformity with the just aspirations of the people. As one index to those aspirations we may consider the Indian National Congress. In regard to this institution we shall find a diversity of opinions prevalent; to the resolutions of the Congress recently held at Madras we have counterblasts from Sir Syud Ahmed, Sir Lepel Griffin, and others. Sir Syud, for himself and on behalf of his co-religionists (the Mahomedans), cannot admit, among other points objected to, that the principle of filling up all appointments by competition, advocated by the Congress, was suitable for India. While contending that the analogy of the English system with respect to the filling up of the Civil Service did not affect the question, because the selected candidates came from a far-off country, &c., Sir Syud has missed the mark. For the credit of Parliamentary Government, I refrain from enlightening him.

Sixty-four years have elapsed since Mountstuart Elphinstone's Minute above referred to, advocating the education of the natives of India to take part in the government of the country, was recorded. For fifty years of that interval the special education in question has been in progress. Nevertheless, the controversy of rival races and creeds, referred to above, in regard to the lines on which a general movement for seeking a share in the government of their country should be drawn, shows that unaided by some impartial master-mind, sympathising with all but bigoted to none, the legitimate aspirations of the people may be retarded to an indefinite period. What time the hour and the man shall arrive must rest with the good sense and moderation of conflicting classes, combining to sink individual jealousies for the attainment of the common good. Meanwhile, let them listen to the final words of Elphinstone, forecasting their high destiny :—

"It may be urged that if we raise the natives to an equality with ourselves by education, and at the same time admit them to a share in their own government, it is not likely that they will be content with the position assigned to them, or will ever rest until they have made good their title to the whole. It cannot be denied that there is much ground for the apprehension; but I do not see that we are at all more secure on any other plan. If we endeavour to depress the natives, our government may be overthrown by their resistance; and such a catastrophe would be more disastrous and more disgraceful than that just supposed. Even if we succeeded in the attempt, our empire being unconnected with the people, would be liable to be subverted either by foreign conquest, or by the revolt of our descendants. And it is better for our honour and interest, as well as for the welfare of mankind, that we should resign our power into the hands of the people for whose benefit it is entrusted, than that it should be wrested from us by a rival nation, or claimed as a birthright by a handful of Creoles."

(Signed) MOUNTSTUART ELPHINSTONE.

SUPPLEMENTARY CHAPTER.

RECURRING now to the allusion in the Preface to the recently-discovered letters of General Lawrence, as throwing light on the miscarriage of my reports in transmission through his office of Agent Governor-General, I may first cite a letter to my address, marginally appended, showing how the earlier reports miscarried. That must of course be accepted as an accident, occasioned, perhaps, by the urgency of the period; and however much to be regretted as precluding the insertion in the Parliamentary Blue

> AJMERE,
> *August 26th*, 1857.
>
> MY DEAR SHOWERS,—I am very sorry to say I have not any of your letters. I must have sent them in as they came, either to the Lieut.-Governor or Mr. Edmonstone. I have searched among all my papers in vain.
>
> (Signed)
> G. L. P. LAWRENCE.

Book of the reports of the opening operations of the Mutiny in one of its principal centres, and of the just tribute paid in the same to the valuable co-operation of the distinguished coadjutors and zealous subordinates with whom it was my good fortune to be associated, the omission of the reports in question was at the time irremediable. But others of the recently discovered letters tell a different tale, and prove, under General Lawrence's own hand, that the statements he made in his letter of the 6th, March, 1876, addressed to Sir John Kaye, and published in the Appendix to the 2nd Edition of Vol. III. of that author's "*History of the Sepoy War*," were contrary to the facts. On becoming aware of the publication of the statements in question, through Colonel Malleson's reference to them in the 1st Vol. of his "History of the Indian Mutiny," purporting to be a re-writing of the history comprised in Kaye's 3rd Vol., I conclusively disposed of the matter at the time by the publication of my correspondence of 1881 with Colonel Malleson* in which I exposed General Lawrence's statements as groundless and self-interested, and animadverted on Colonel Malleson's lending countenance to them by suppressing, in his re-writing of Kaye's 3rd volume, an important incident of the period related by that author which practically refuted them. General Lawrence, then alive, did not venture to attempt to justify his statements, or to repel my charges, nor did Colonel Malleson either on behalf of his hero or for himself, venture upon any rejoinder. To Colonel Malleson and his histories I need here no further return or refer, having already broken that prolific compositor on the wheel of historic honour and truth; and I willingly take leave of one who writes histories—ancient, mediæval, modern, and contemporary,—with

* "Indian History and Colonel Malleson, C.S.I. By Major-General C. L. Showers. London: Reeves and Turner, 1881."

the air of a Polybius, a Cæsar, or a Napier, whilst in reality

> "He never set a squadron in the field,
> Nor the division of a battle knew, more than a spinster."

And now turn up letters, under General Lawrence's own hand, directly arraigning him for unaccountable misrepresentation in respect of the statements in question. The apparent influencing motive of such misrepresentation will appear presently. The letters in question it is now necessary to set forth in counter columns:—

From Lieut.-General GEO. LAWRENCE to Sir JOHN KAYE.
Dated,
KENSINGTON PARK GARDENS.
6th March, 1876.

MY DEAR KAYE,—I wish to call your attention to a statement in the third volume of your "History of the Sepoy Mutiny," in reference to my proceedings in Rajputana during that crisis. You say, "It was not a propitious circumstance that George "Lawrence, who had preceded "Showers as Political Agent at "Oodeypore, had been involved "in a sharp conflict with the "Meywar Durbar (Oodeypore) "and had recommended Military

From Colonel GEO. LAWRENCE to Captain SHOWERS.
Dated, CAMP GUNERAO,
4th March, 1857.

Acknowledges letter of 27th February preceding.

. . . . The Oodeypore Despatch Letter Book will make you acquainted with the present state of affairs. . . . The Saloombra man's Vakeel" (this refers to one of the chief nobles of Oodeypore) "has not been near me for a long time . . . . I would suggest that if Saloombra sends his to you, that you desire him to return without seeing him, and say that his case is now "coercion, the deposition of the "Maharana, and the banishment "of some of the principal Chiefs "under him. Whether right or "wrong, the tendency of this "policy might have been to "alienate the confidence, if not "to excite the hostility of the "Meywar Durbar in this con- "juncture. But Showers, the "Political Agent, met the Maha- "rana, and, according to his own "statement, prevailed on him to "give his open adhesion to the "British cause, and to place the "most trustworthy troops at his "disposal to take the field."

The fact is I never had any conflict at all with the Maharana, never recommended his deposition, nor any military coercion with regard to him. Sir H. Lawrence and I had, in 1855, advocated the coercion by British troops of some of the Meywar nobles, and even if necessary the deposition of the principal one, the Rawat of Saloombra, and to this I think you must be referring. But these measures were for the support of the Maharana's authority, and in conjunction with him, and in 1857 I was, as I had ever been, and as I continued to be, always on terms of confidential intimacy with him.

(Signed)

G. L. P. LAWRENCE.

before Government. *The Rana too, you will observe, is in my black books.* (The italics are mine.—C. L. S.) Please watch his conduct to Shere Singh, the Minister, who has our guarantee against being ill-treated.

(Signed)

G. L. P. LAWRENCE.

The misrepresentation as to General Lawrence not having ever had any conflict with the Maharana, but on the contrary being in 1857, as he had ever been, on terms of confidential intimacy with him, is here established under his own hand. Moreover, the cause of the difference so absolutely denied, is rendered abundantly intelligible by the words following the announcement of the fact that "the Rana was in his 'black books,'" viz.: "Please watch his conduct to Shere Singh, the minister, who has our guarantee against being ill-treated." Herein stands revealed the cause of offence on both sides. The Maharana, on the one hand—a sovereign prince guaranteed by treaty against all interference with his internal administration—naturally felt umbrage at his servant intriguing, and successfully, to get the British Resident's support against himself, his sovereign lord and master; and he punished the offending Minister, as it was his indefeasible right to do, by dismissing him from office and degrading him at Court. General Lawrence, on the other hand, unadmonished by such significant incident of the error into which he had fallen, resented his Highness' assertion of his sovereign authority over his own servant as an act of defiance; and accordingly, to use his own words, placed the Prince on his "black books."

To have followed Colonel Lawrence's lead as expressly given in the injunction to "watch the Maharana's conduct to Shere Singh, the Minister," would undoubtedly have smoothed my current official course. But Justice and Public Policy forbade. In the first place it would have been supporting a breach of treaty engagement under which the protected Princes of India were guaranteed against any interference in their internal administration. In respect to this the appointment and dismissal of their own Ministers was, as a matter of course, the most primary right. In the next place, it was certain to give grievous umbrage to the

Maharana, and thus destroy the confidence and friendly understanding that should subsist between a British Resident and the Sovereign of the Court to which he is accredited. The history of British India teems with examples of clever intriguing Ministers trying to get on the shoulders of their legitimate lords and masters by ingratiating themselves with, and acquiring undue influence over incautious Political Officers. Impressed with this lesson, and being satisfied that in the case in question Maharana Soroop Singh was in no way to blame for asserting his independence in the way he had done, my sense of justice precluded my making any change, on resuming my post as Resident at his court, in the friendly relations that had formerly subsisted between us when I was officiating Resident in Meywar seven years previous. Public Policy further at that juncture dictated, in my opinion, as a point of very especial importance, the maintenance of friendly relations with the most powerful Hindoo Prince in India, having reference to the near approach of the Mutiny. Having placed on record at the Board of Control, India Office, before leaving England the previous year, my apprehension of a revolt in India as the consequence of the series of annexations of Native States, especially Oude, the home and recruiting field of the Bengal Army, I recognised in the incipient mutinies of detached regiments here and there, the incendiarisms at various stations, the circulation of secret signs, etc., during the latter months of 1856 and beginning of 1857, the near approach of the coming storm. Moved, therefore, by considerations at once of justice and true policy, I met the Maharana on taking charge of my office with my usual cordiality, and resumed my official intercourse with him with the same friendly confidence as before. As for the late Minister, Mehta Shere Singh, I could not recognise the guarantee so injudiciously given to him against the Maharana by Colonel Lawrence. Having been dismissed from office by his legitimate lord and master, he was dead to me. Though well acquainted personally with the Mehtajee, as he was familiarly called, and aware of his ability, I studiously avoided the mention of his name or any reference to the change in His Highness's ministerial arrangements. The good effects of this policy were strikingly manifested, when the Mutiny broke out within a month, in the signal services which His Highness rendered to the British cause at that crisis. These have been detailed in the course of the preceding narrative—services which drew from Her Majesty the Queen, speaking through her Secretary of State, the expression of her "highest gratification in observing the support which he gave to her armies, the assistance which he rendered to her subjects, and the tranquillity he maintained throughout his extensive dominions; and assuring His Highness that these proofs of his loyalty and devotion to the British Crown would ever be held by Her Majesty in grateful remembrance." General Lawrence, in his letter to Sir John Kaye, adverted to this well-merited tribute and complacently took credit for it. Here we arrive at an understanding of the motive above referred to, influencing his misrepresentation of the fact in regard to his relations with Maharana Soroop Singh. Had General Lawrence stopped there he would have been welcome to his version—the sense of having fearlessly done my duty in so momentous a crisis, and the grateful acknowledgments of those benefitted by my exertions, being my all-sufficing reward. But when, in reference to Kaye's strictures on the manifest injustice of his ignoring, in his official report, my conspicuous action in the field, General Lawrence attempted to justify his own conduct herein by the romance he invented, he necessitated my exposing and denouncing, through the publication of my correspondence of 1881 with his advocate (Colonel Malleson), his "interested depreciation of my services."

His suppression, after the foregoing examples of his imaginative faculty and fairplay, of all reference to the Secretary of State's despatch, on appeal, and my consequent restoration to office, while citing the original despatch of the subordinate Local Government removing me for acting without orders, goes without saying.

The ground of the Secretary of State's favorable decision may be shortly gathered from the concluding paragraph of my memorial in appeal, dated 19th February, 1862.

"15. The last point which I would respectfully submit, in conclusion, has reference to the question of responsibility, involving, as it appears to my humble judgment, an important principle of administration. It is admitted that the responsibility I assumed in the attack on Neembahera was at a crisis of great public difficulty and danger. It has been proved, both by the testimony of the highest political authority on the spot and corroborated by the patent and undisputed event, that my responsible action in question achieved a success which was attended with important public advantage. I would here humbly, and with all deference, submit to the Secretary of State in Council, whether the whole course of British history does not point to full indemnity, at least, having been invariably granted to successful achievements under similar circumstances."

General Lawrence's statement was not only practically refuted by the event, as exhibited, but further confuted, under his own hand, in the very first letter he addressed to me through his amanuensis, Dr. Ebden, the Residency Surgeon, after rejoining my post at Oodeypore. This letter has only now turned up along with the others above quoted, and, as conveying Sir H. Lawrence's dying message to the Maharana, will be read with a painful interest. It is dated Aboo, 1st June, 1857, and runs as follows :—

"From Dr. EBDEN,

"Dated Rajputana Agency, Aboo,

"2 p.m., June 1st, 1857.

"MY DEAR SHOWERS,

"Colonel Lawrence has received your letter of the 30th May" [from Oodeypore, where I had already rejoined my post two days previously. C. L. S.]. "He feels sure that you will do all that is necessary and best. . . . . The Colonel deems your advice to the Gagoonda Rao" [one of the most powerful Meywar Chiefs, through whose territories my route lay in returning from Aboo to Oodeypore] "most judicious and excellent, and he hopes earnestly that the Rao will act on it.

"Please tell the Rana that Sir Henry has written from Lucknow: 'Tell the Rana of Meywar that NOW is the time and hour for him to earn favour and a good name with our Government, even if it cost him lakhs of rupees, for money spent now will fructify well.'

"Yours very sincerely,

(Signed) "H. EBDEN.

"To Captain CHARLES SHOWERS,

"Oodeypore, etc., etc."

Sir Henry Lawrence held the reversionary appointment of Governor-General, to provide against contingencies at the crisis of the Mutiny, when he was killed at Lucknow. Well might that sagacious statesman, in that hour of supreme peril, tremble at the thought of the most powerful Hindoo Prince in India and traditional Head of all, having been alienated to the last extremity, and with his dying breath invoke His Highness's aid in our cause. The object of his appeal, however, had happily been already anticipated. And since it was my good fortune to be the humble instrument of conciliating and enlisting that vital support, I desire to ascribe the credit of it to my late honoured chief, Sir Henry, as it was on his recommendation to Lord Canning that I was appointed to the Meywar Residency at that critical conjuncture.

THE END.

APPENDIX.

APPENDIX.

(Copy).

No. 267, of 1857.

To BRIGADIER-GENERAL G. LAWRENCE,

Officiating Agent Governor-General for the States of Rajputana.

Dated NEEMUCH, 8*th November*, 1857, 10 *p.m.*

SIR,—In continuation of my letter of this morning's date, I have the honour to report for your information that the rebel force advanced to the attack of Neemuch to-day. On hearing of their approach, the Cavalry under Captain Bannister and the Meywar Horse under myself moved out and met the rebels about a mile or two from Cantonments. They formed up in line on our approach, about 4 p.m., seemingly in number about 2,000 with many Standards and Cavalry on the advance and rear-guard, and opened fire from three guns. After keeping the rebels in check for an hour or so, the regular Cavalry was retired under general restrictive orders, as it appeared, from Captain Simpson, who, you will have learnt from my despatch of this morning, had assumed Command of the Troops while still unable to take the field with them. Perceiving the rebels then moving towards the town of Neemuch, I moved forward with the Meywar Irregulars and headed them. They halted and opened fire again but with no effect, beyond one officer's (Lieut. Stapleton) horse shot under him; and thus they were held in check till dark, when I withdrew the main body of the troops, leaving pickets to protect the rear of Cantonments Had the bulk of the force been moved out to-day with our guns, a complete success over the rebels would, in my opinion, have attended our operations; that is, if they had been conducted without reference to restrictive orders from a Commandant not in the field. It remains to be seen what measures will be taken to-morrow.

I have, &c.,

(Signed) C. L. SHOWERS,

Officiating Resident, Meywar States.

NEEMUCH, 8*th November*, 1857.

(Copy).

No. 202A, of 1857.

From BRIGADIER-GENERAL G. LAWRENCE,
Officiating Agent Governor-General for the States of Rajputana.
To CAPTAIN C. L. SHOWERS,
Officiating Resident in Meywar.

Dated AJMERE, *12th November*, 1857.

SIR,—I have the honour to acknowledge the receipt of your letters of the 7th and 8th instant, reporting the advance of the rebel force from Mundisore to the attack of Neemuch, and in reply to inform you that I consider Captain Simpson used a sound discretion in not risking his handful of Infantry and 2 guns against an enemy "seemingly in number about 2,000;" as any reverse would, in all probability, have involved the loss of the Fortified Square and destruction of all the Force.

I have, &c.,

(Signed) G. S. P. LAWRENCE,
Officiating Agent Governor-General.

Rajputana Agency, AJMERE, *12th November*, 1857.

CAMP IN THE FIELD,
10th November (Tuesday).

MY DEAR SIR,—The rebels having attacked Neemuch, I write to request you to move on with all dispatch with the ammunition. The Hakim of Chitore will be directed to afford you every assistance, as also the Superintendent of Neembahera. At this latter post I will either meet your party, or have a strong escort in readiness to strengthen your own. All the cavalry of the Neemuch force is in the field, and will join.

The rebels attacked the station on the evening of the 8th, but were kept in check all that night. The next morning, as there was no move out against them by the Neemuch force, they came in unobstructed, and burnt what was left of the station and attacked the fort. Their heavy guns came up only yesterday.

By a note from the fort at 7 a.m. this morning, nobody was hurt.

Believe me,

Yours faithfully,

C. L. SHOWERS.

To Capt. Baumgartner,
Commanding Detachment.

To SECRETARY EDMONSTONE, ESQ.,

Dated Camp in the field, Neembahera,

11th November, 1857.

In advertence to the advantage that has already been experienced by us at this critical juncture from the possession of Neembahera as a British post, I trust I may be excused in drawing attention to this early demonstration of the beneficial results of the policy that dictated its occupation. Had Neembahera remained in the hands of the Tonk authorities, the chief of whom proceeded straight to Mundisore and joined openly the Mahomedan movements against us which he was suspected to be secretly fomenting in his own circle, there can be no doubt that instead of the Neemuch garrison having its rear secured and communication open, and the Cavalry in the field a strong post in the vicinity of the rebels from whence operations to harass the latter can be undertaken, Neembahera would have become on the occasion of the inroad of the Mundisore rebels, the focus of another hostile movement in our rear in furtherance of the crusade preached by the fanatic Shahzada against the British.

I am enabled to communicate daily with the Fort. All well, and no one hurt except two officers slightly hit by spent balls.

(Signed) C. L. SHOWERS.

NUSSERABAD,

18th June.

MY DEAR SHOWERS,—Both your letters of the 15th have duly arrived; that written last came first. As the General is at present here, I sent them both to him, and I shall send the horsemen who take back this to him also, that they may take you his answer.

I am uncertain whether the General intends sending any of us in pursuit of the mutineers, but I think he will not. Situated as we are here, I quite agree with him that it would be the height of imprudence to risk the safety of Ajmere, which depends entirely on our presence here; so much so, that I expect our absence for even a week would raise all the ill-disposed about the country.

(Signed) HENRY MACAN.

SECRET CORRESPONDENCE

RELATING TO THE CRISIS, CONFIDED BY MAHARANA SOROOP SINGH TO CAPTAIN SHOWERS, THE RESIDENT, FOR SUBMISSION TO THE GOVERNOR-GENERAL.

(Copy).

No. 51 of 1858.

From CAPTAIN C. L. SHOWERS,
Officiating Political Resident, Meywar.

To BRIGADIER-GENERAL G. S. P. LAWRENCE,
Officiating Resident Governor-General for the States of Rajputanah.

Dated, OODEYPORE, 21*st February*, 1858.

Secret Department.

SIR,—I have the honour to forward for your information and for submission to the Right Honorable the Governor-General in Council, the accompanying copies, with translation of certain papers which have been confided to me by the Muha Rana of Oodeypore bearing intimately on the present crisis in India. Government have already had before them many proofs referred to in my previous reports of His Highness's fidelity and friendship throughout this period. The papers now submitted serve to show that besides individual attachment on the part of himself and his State, influencing immediately by his example the subordinate States under the Meywar Residency, the Rana has exerted his great influence as the acknowledged Head of all the Rajpoot Princes, on the side of the British by advising all who applied to him by letter or by accredited ministers specially deputed, for counsel at the crisis which had seemed to have cut them off from their accustomed protector and left them at the mercy of formidable armed bands of rebels and licentious mutinous soldiery, by advising all at that momentous juncture to stand firm in their allegiance to the British Government; counsel which was recommended to their adoption by his own high example.

The Papers here submitted comprise:—

1st. A correspondence between the Rewah Rajah and the Muha Ranah (marked A in Appendix). Premising that the former is closely connected with the Oodeypore House by marriage to strengthen the sentiment of traditional fealty to the Muha Rana which attach him in common with all the Rajpoot Princes, the Rewah Rajah's first letter, it will be observed, was dated 11th June last (1857). To which the Muha Rana replied on the 15th August. "Through the good fortune of the Sirkar (paramount power) it is hoped that everything will speedily be settled. The advent of the British power has proved beneficial to all the chiefs in Rajwara, and has been the means of restoring tranquillity to the country. On this account we earnestly wish and pray to Sreejee (the deity) for the stability of the British power. I hope you will bear in mind what I have here written."

The Rewah Rajah wrote again on the 20th August, it will be observed (before the letter from the Rana above quoted could have been received), wherein, adverting to passing events, Rewah placed himself and his troops at the Muha Rana's disposal in the following terms: "whatever you have decided upon I am ready to do the same. Write me your advice on this head as early as possible. I look up to no one else for advice but yourself in the present crisis. I cannot write more. Myself and my troops are at your disposal."

In reply to this it will be further observed the Muha Rana wrote, referring the Rewah Rajah to his former letter, and urging him to active efforts in our favour, in addition to his previous counsel to stand firm and to take example by him. "It is therefore the duty of every one of us to afford every assistance to the British Government. I advise you to bear this in mind and follow my example."

3. When this last communication was written, dated 13th November, the British garrison and post of Neemuch was besieged by the rebels. The Pergunnah capitals of the British district of Jawud Neemuch had thrown off their allegiance and declared for

the rebel Shahzada. The British Native Cavalry in the field intent only on retreat out of Meywar, notwithstanding my repeated remonstrances, and only checked by the advance of the Mhow column, although its retreat would have left me entirely dependent on the Meywar troops in the field.

4. The Rewah Rajah, I believe, in all the difficulties by which he has been surrounded, stood alone amid faltering officials and mutinous troops in his staunchness to the British, and his support of the Political Resident. It will remain with His Lordship the Governor-General, after perusal of this correspondence, to judge how far the Rajah was influenced for good by the advice and example of his relative and acknowledged Head of the Rajpoot clans, the Muha Rana of Oodeypore.

5. The next paper of the file is the memorandum (marked B in Appendix). It relates, it will be observed, to the mission of an accredited minister on the part of the Jodhpore Rajah Tukht Singh to Oodeypore to seek counsel from the Muha Ranah, with an intimation that his master was prepared to act as the Ranah did or desired. That the powerful State of Jodhpore, equally with the other Rajpoot States, acknowledged the Muha Ranah of Oodeypore as the common Head, is shown by the appended extracts of Khureetas (marked F) from the former sovereigns of that state, including also addresses from all of the other principal Rajpoot States. The answer returned to Rajah Tukht Singh by the Ranah of Oodeypore was to the same effect as that given to the Rewah Rajah, advising him to stand firm by the British Government.

6. The date of this mission from Jodhpore may appear to the Governor-General as worthy of especial notice on account of the following concomitant circumstances. The mission arrived at Oodeypore, it will be observed, on the 8th October, and may therefore be supposed (calculating the distance) to have been despatched from Jodhpore in consequence of the difficulties in which Rajah Tukht Singh found himself plunged by the failure of the attack on Ahwa by the British troops in concert with the defeat of his own, aggravated by the loss of the British Political Resident in the same affair. This event occurred on the 20th September.

7. On the same day by a singular coincidence Neembahera was

occupied by the successful military operations of the force from Neemuch. I have in previous despatches had occasion to advert to the compensating sedative effect of this measure, especially when bringing under notice on the part of my assistant in the hilly tract the danger to the public tranquillity in Meywar which had arisen from the temporary success of the Ahwa chief in rebellion, owing to the bond of union from clanship and identity of class interests between the recusant chiefs in both these contiguous states, and the force of which bond has now been the more conclusively demonstrated by many of the Ahwa fugitives having been suffered to pass unchallenged through the estates of some of the chiefs in Meywar, and have found refuge, it is believed, within the bounds of one of the most powerful of them. An intercepted correspondence between Ahwa and Suloomber near about the date of this mission from Jodhpore, and which has been placed in my hands by the Durbar, exhibits a further and so conclusive a proof of intimate connexion between these chiefs as to afford a strong ground for the assumption that, but for the change of attitude on the part of the British force at Neemuch, marching boldly out and capturing a strong place at a moment when it was supposed to be cooped up in its entrenchments awaiting succour, that but for this sign of reviving power to our arms Suloomber might have been tempted to openly join the Marwar Thakoors. That chief, the head of so powerful a party in the state, once committed, we might have expected a flame in Meywar which, uniting with the insurrections in Marwar on the one side, Kotah on the other, and the Mahomedan movement in Malwa and in the heart of our districts of Jawud Neemuch, the combination moreover finding us with wavering Native troops within our own camp, and a post unfurnished with the necessary magazine,—I need hardly point to the probable consequence for the time of such a state of things, temporary although in reference to the ultimate issue it must have been. In contrast with what might have happened I would beg to point out what has obtained. Suloomber, though more than once, as you are aware, on the point of breaking out, has never ventured to do so, Meywar has remained internally tranquil. The balance between faltering states has been maintained.

The saving effect of the service and success at Neembahera upon the wavering Native troops at Neemuch, has been exhibited in the proofs submitted in my despatches to your address noted in margin.

To Officiating Resident Governor-General, Rajpootana, dated 28th September, 1857.
To do. No. 286, dated 2nd December, 1857.
To. do. No. 20, dated 22nd January, 1858.
To do. No. 34, dated 5th February, 1858.

8. The next paper in the file (marked C) is copy of a circular which was proposed by the Muha Ranah, and after communication with me addressed by His Highness to all the Tankadar Rajpoot Chiefs under the Neemuch Superintendency, and which were forwarded by me before the Neemuch troops rose, under cover to Captain Lloyd, the Superintendent, for transmission to the Chiefs should he deem expedient. Thus, when the revolt took place on 3rd June, and some of the British officers and families sought refuge in some of these Chiefships, all such were sheltered and protected. To account for the influence exercised by the Rana's addresses to these Tankadar Chiefs, it may perhaps be necessary to explain briefly the connexion between them. These Chiefs being scions of the Rana's own family, four of them even classed among the thirty-two hereditary Sirdars of the Oodeypore State and Nobles of the Court, and having received their titles and estates as such, the general sentiment of loyalty with which other Rajpoot clans look up to the Rana as the HINDOO PUT, naturally operates with double force upon these Chiefs who are bound to him by family ties as, at once, the Head of their House, and their sometime Sovereign. The salutary effect of the Rana's influence over these Chiefs under the Neemuch Superintendency, His Lordship the Governor-General may perhaps be the better able to judge of, when their loyal conduct is placed in contrast with that of all the other chief towns of the district which threw off the allegiance of the British Government by receiving officers appointed by the new rebel King who had established himself in Central India.

9. The paper (marked D) is copy of a general Proclamation

issued by the Muha Rana on the 27th May, on my requisition, calling upon all the Chiefs of the State to send their quotas of troops to aid our operations. Thereby was secured the active co-operation which enabled me to pursue the Neemuch mutineers, clear the post-road, bring up a body of Native troops to the Ajmere frontier to co-operate with the Nusseerabad force for the destruction of the revolted brigade, on a plan previously submitted by express for your consideration—further, to occupy and hold the post of Neemuch, when not only denuded of British troops, but in the presence of mutinous Kotah troops. By that Proclamation, further, was secured that active personal assistance on the part of some of the Chiefs, including the highest, which resulted in the relief and escorting, to a place of safety, of all the women, children, and sick of the Neemuch garrison. Such confidence had I in the efficacy of the Rana's Proclamation, in conjunction with my own issued at the same time in communication with His Highness, that on relieving one party of the Neemuch refugees in the vicinity of the desolated station, I consigned them, that is the women, children, and sick of of the party, unhesitatingly to the care of the Rao of Bedla, the highest Chief of Oodeypore who had taken the field with me, and left him to escort them to Oodeypore while I myself proceeded in pursuit of the mutineers. How well he discharged that important trust is known to His Lordship the Governor-General who has conveyed to His Highness the Muha Rana, his thanks for the protection afforded to the refugees. The rest of the Neemuch garrison were escorted in safety to Nusseerabad by another party of the Rana's troops under a Durbar officer at a time when all Malwa had just risen, the mutineers from Mhow, Indore and Augur, were on the road, and Meywar lying in their most direct route to their destination, Delhee. None of the party was injured or molested in their progress through the wild tract of country between Neemuch and Nusseerabad. Thus all of the garrison were rescued and placed in safety.

A further good effect (of the Proclamation) that may be here cited has reference to the uninterrupted transit of the post through Meywar, after it was re-opened by our chasing the Neemuch mutineers off the road immediately after the mutiny. The import nce of this point will be the better appreciated by Government when it is remembered that the route through Meywar was, in the general closing of all the other post lines by insurrection, for some time and that the most critical, the only channel of communication between Government, even the supreme Government as well as the Government of Bombay, with the North Western Provinces, then the seat of War, and all the intermediate stations. This channel of communication has never been interrupted for a day in the Meywar States throughout the whole period of the troubled times.

10. Appendix (E) is a communication from the Kotah Rajah to the Muha Rana of Oodeypore, on the occasion of the revolt of his troops and murder of the British Resident. The Rajah would appear to have applied to the Muha Ranah for advice, at the juncture, equally as the Head of Rajpoot Chiefs, and more particularly as being nearly connected by marriage, the Kotah Rajah being married to a daughter of the Oodeypore House. His Highness, immediately on receipt of the letter from Kotah, communicated the fact to me through his minister. His advice to the Rajah, it will be observed, was not to allow what had happened to induce him to commit himself with the English Government. The Muha Ranah wished to bring away and receive his relation, the Kotah Ranee at Oodeypore, or at least to afford her refuge within his territories as the privacy of the Kotah Zenana was hardly secure from the assault of the rebellious troops on the palace. But considering that the Ranee could only come with a large retinue from Kotah, I thought it better that the Muha Ranah should not be mixed up in Kotah affairs at such a time, and suggested that he should leave them to decide upon some other place of retreat, when His Highness gave up the point. The Kotah Rajah's desire to state his case to me through the Muha Ranah I declined to entertain, and a Khureeta to my address from the Muha Rao of Kotah I returned unopened.

11. The only other incident touching the Muha Rana's relations with other Princes in India, that I have to bring under notice, as bearing on the crisis (besides his near connection with Bikaneer and Jesulmere, the former of which has co-operated so actively on our side) has reference to a proposal His Highness made to me in personal conference in the first days of June, at the outburst of

the insurrection, to write to the Nipal Rajah, as being a junior branch of the Oodeypore House, in view to bringing about a combined movement in our favour, between the Nipalese and all the other Rajpoot States. The two Princes are descended, as you are aware, from a common ancestor. Two of the Nipaul Sirdars are at the present time in attendance at the Oodeypore Durbar. But on reflection I considered the time too critical and pregnant with hourly change in events to encourage the proposal. I have thought it right, however, to mention the incident as affording one more instance of the Rana's thoughtful earnestness in our cause, and as regarding that of all the Rajpoot Princes as identified with it. It will rest with His Lordship the Governor-General to judge in what degree, if any, the Nipal Rajah may have been influenced in his recent active co-operation in the field with our troops, by the example from the first and urgent injunctions to other Rajpoot Princes of their common Head, and in respect of Nipal, the senior representative of their common ancestor.

12. The Muha Rana, in confiding to my judgment the delicate matters involved in the correspondence he placed in my hands, expressed a natural hope that the circumstance of some of the Princes having sought his counsel, as their traditional head, at this critical juncture when surrounded by danger, and cut off from the accustomed protection of the British Government, might not be imputed to their disadvantage as an indication of a wavering spirit in their loyalty to the Paramount Power.

13. The faithful and friendly conduct of Muha Rana Suroop Singh, of Oodeypore, as further illustrated by the papers and facts herewith submitted in continuation of previous reports, I have thought it my duty, as the Officer accredited to His Highness Court, to lay before His Lordship in Council, and having acquitted myself of this duty towards at once the Rana and my own Government, I should under ordinary circumstances have considered that I had done enough, and would gladly have left it to my official superiors to judge of the degree of credit, that in their indulgence might be allowed to attach to my management of Meywar affairs. But since your review of my official proceedings has mostly been, I regret to think, of a character to place me on my defence, I may,

perhaps, be permitted, in justice to myself, to draw the attention of Government to the circumstances under which I received charge of the Office in March last (1857), just previous to which the disposition of the Muha Rana on the one hand, equally with that of some of the highest chiefs on the other, had been represented as so obstructive as to induce the late Agent Governor-General to recommend to Government that a strong force should march into Meywar specially to coerce all parties. And without exposing myself to the charge of assumption or egotism, I may be further permitted, I trust, to point to the proofs herein submitted, in continuation of former instances of the Rana's favourable disposition towards our Government, exhibited under my guidance, not only without the presence of an extraordinary armed force, but at a crisis of temporary weakness (whereby in view of a similar disposition manifested by all the other States under this Agency), His Lordship may judge of my administration in Meywar.

I have, &c.,

(Signed) C. L. SHOWERS,

Officiating Political Resident.

Meywar Agency, OODEYPORE, 21*st February*, 1858.

(TRUE COPY).

(Signed) C. L. SHOWERS,

Officiating Political Resident.

MEMORANDUM.—The documents referred to in this despatch, filed in original in the Meywar Residency Office, and translations forwarded as enclosures to the same.

(Signed) C. L. SHOWERS.

THE REDUCTION OF THE NATIVE ARMIES OF INDIA.

TO THE EDITOR OF "THE TIMES."

SIR,—Your recent articles on the reduction of the native armies of India, equally British and belonging to the native States, raise an important question to the discussion of which I would beg a brief space in *The Times* to add my humble contribution. The assumption in passing, may be conceded—that the results of the present war in Afghanistan will find us, on the conclusion of a satisfactory peace, with a frontier so strengthened in the north-west boundary of India that we may with safety, and with manifest advantage to the relief on the Indian finances, considerably reduce our native army; and you urge, with much *primâ facie* show of reason, that the native States, protected by the British Power from all external danger, might simultaneously reduce their armies, the existence of which in their present strength would otherwise prove a source of danger to us under our reduced armament. The remainder of the troops retained by the States you think might expediently be maintained on the footing of British contingents—officered, it is presumed, by British officers, like those now in existence—supporting this opinion on the ground that the States profess themselves ready to place their troops at the disposal of the Indian Government as often as their services may be called for; *ergo*, accept the offer once for all *en permanence*.

The question has three sides—(1) as regards the British troops stationed in the territories of the native States; (2) as regards that portion of the armies of some of the States which is composed of foreign mercenaries and is maintained and organised exclusively as a standing army; and (3) as regards that portion which is composed of the feudal retainers of the Princes, augmented on occasions of war, or of military ceremonials, such as the Derserah festival, by the aggregate number of the rétainers of the assembled chiefs, whose presence in attendance on their suzerain is *de rigueur* on such occasions.

With respect to the first side of the question, I have long been of opinion that the quartering of British forces in the territories of the native States generally was unnecessary, and in a despatch to the address of the Foreign Secretary, so long ago as 1867, I submitted grounds to show that those stationed in Rajputana at least—the field from which my examples from personal knowledge were more immediately cited—might be withdrawn with safety. My views on this head have been fortified by the recently-published opinion of Sir Bartle Frere in his letters to the address of Sir John Kaye, under date June 12, 1874, and January 11, 1875. I cited the following instances in proof that the native States not only did not require British troops to watch them, but, on the contrary, that they could be of material aid to the British Government in periods of public danger on the one hand or of internal difficulty on the other; in cases where, from the nature of the country and the character of the object to be attained, British troops, with their impedimenta, could not operate with any hope of success. The first instance cited was the suppression of the great marauding system that ravaged Western India in the years 1846-7. The formidable character of the movement was attested by the exploits of the band—first, in the forcible rescue of one of their imprisoned comrades from the central gaol of Agra, and next, in the attack and successful plunder of the Government treasury at Nusseerabad, both stations being military garrisons. A force was ordered to take the field to punish the outrage on our authority and put down the movement; but the contemplated employment of regulars was overruled by the Political Resident in favour of operations by the troops of the native States exclusively, placed under my command as his military *attaché*. Those operations, owing mainly to the hearty co-operation of the States, were entirely successful, resulting in the capture of the outlawed chief with his principal followers after a harassing pursuit under my immediate command into the heart of the great western desert and assault on his stronghold. Thus quiet was restored to the country and the authority of Government vindicated without the necessity of a desert campaign, necessarily costly at any rate and the issue in the circumstances obviously doubtful. The next instance cited was the effective assistance which the States rendered us, during the preparations for the Punjab war of 1848-49, in furnishing supplies of carriage, food, grain, &c. The third instance was the furnishing of a contingent to take the field in the same war under my command. The last instance cited was the aid afforded by the ruler of Oodeypore on the outbreak of the Mutiny of 1857, in furnishing me with a body of his household troops for the rescue of the Neemuch refugees, and, subsequently, in various ways throughout the troubled times. Government on every occasion cordially acknowledged the services rendered by the States. On the last cited the Maharana of Oodeypore was honoured by the gracious acknowledgements of Her Imperial Majesty the Queen. The troops employed on all the occasions above cited were exclusively *feudal retainers* of the different States concerned.

The second side of the question relates to the foreign mercenaries maintained as a standing army by some of the States. Here, I agree with you, is an element of possible danger which, as necessitating the presence or proximity of British troops in observation, might expediently be reduced in amicable negotiation with the rulers of the States concerned—not as implying in the remotest degree distrust of the existing rulers, but to guard against possible complications in the event of contingencies, the force of which consideration the sensible Princes in question would doubtless recognize. With this provision the reduction of the British Native Army by the aggregate force maintained in the territories of the native States at large would afford material relief to the Army Estimates.

With respect to the third side of the question, having reference to that portion of the native armies which is composed of the retainers of the Princes and of their chiefs, I would earnestly deprecate the measure mooted of converting these bodies into numerically reduced British contingents. It would be so fundamentally opposed to the feudal constitution under which these States subsist that its introduction, I conceive, would not be practicable, except by the total subversion of the States themselves. And, again, even if it were possible to effect the change the vast subsidiary system which would thus be created might be expected, from the experience of the past, to prove utterly unreliable for our defensive purposes, and, on the contrary, dangerous to our power if ever threatened from any quarter or cause, external or internal.

In the first place, the presence of a body of retainers in the Courts of the native States, and even at the chiefships of the subordinate feudatories, is considered essential to the dignity and status generally of all the aristocracy of the States in their several degrees. I may cite one striking example which passed under my own eyes to show the tenacity with which the feudal privilege of maintaining retainers is held. Maharana Soroop Singh of Oodeypore tried, as a means of increasing his revenues, to commute the feudal personal service of his chief's retainers, in the proportion to which he was entitled, into money payments, waiving their attendance. But the chiefs banded themselves together in a league of rebellion to resist such an encroachment on their privileges, and the Maharana had to abandon the attempt. But supposing, for the sake of argument, in the second place, the change effected, and in place of the native retainers a British contingent at each Court or within each territory, irrespective of the repugnance with which such a change would be regarded by the Princes generally, what might be expected of the conduct of the contingents if tested in the crucible of public danger? Let the history of the great Mutiny answer. Nearly all the contingents revolted, many of them killing their officers. The Gwalior contingent, numbering some 10,000 strong, the best paid and equipped of all the native troops of their class throughout India, and distributed throughout some half dozen stations, all went—the Kotah contingent, the Mahidpore contingent, the Jodhpore legion, the Bhopal contingent, &c. Now, it may be asked, what inherent defect is there in the subsidiary system that, as a rule, renders it so unreliable in the vital point of fidelity to the commanders of its legions. I answer, the fact of the knowledge of the men that they are eating the salt of one party while commanded by another. Fidelity to his salt is the highest honour of man in all stages of society. In the lower grade of the military mercenary among the natives of India the feeling is intensified by the terrors of superstition. Namuk-harâm! (faithless to thy salt!) is the last reproach among Orientals.

You say well, in rating the strength of the native armies at 300,000, "but these are broken up into a number of small forces, among at least 40 States and little principalities which have never been able to unite, and by their very geographical position are unable to do so." Herein I quite agree with you. Let us, then, only so order our rule in India in relation to the native States that, since all history exhibits them as owning nominal allegiance to some suzerain, they shall feel that the just and tolerant protectorate of the British is the best possible condition under which they could subsist, when, as in the great Akbar's time 300 years ago, and in our own of yesterday, so in the future, the brave retainers of our faithful feudatories will ever be found ready to defend our cause and, as identified with it, their own.

I am, Sir, yours faithfully,

C. L. SHOWERS, Major-General.

LAHORE,
March 20.

LORD DALHOUSIE'S MINUTES ON THE SATARA SUCCESSION QUESTION.

30*th August*, 1848.

Para. 3 "I am clearly of opinion that the death of His Highness Shreemunt Maharaj without heirs natural having rendered the throne of Satara vacant, that territory should be held, in accordance with practice and with law, to have lapsed to the paramount State, and should henceforth be incorporated with the British territories in India."

Para. 22. "I am unable to admit the force of the argument advanced by Sir George Clerk for its continuance, which is founded on the happy and prosperous condition of the State, and the just and praiseworthy government of the late Rajah."

Para. 25. "I take this fitting occasion of recording my strong and deliberate opinion, that in the exercise of a wise and sound policy, the British Government is bound not to put aside or to neglect such rightful opportunities of acquiring territory or revenue as may from time to time present themselves, whether they rise from the lapse of subordinate States, by the failure of all heirs of every description whatsoever, or from the failure of heirs natural, when the succession can be sustained only by the sanction of government being given to the ceremony of adoption according to Hindoo Law."

Para. 29. "There may be conflict of opinion as to the advantage or the propriety of extending our already vast possessions beyond their present limits. . . . But I cannot conceive it possible for any one to dispute the policy of taking advantage of every just opportunity which presents itself for consolidating the territories which already belong to us, by taking possession of States which may lapse in the midst of them; for thus getting rid of these petty intruding principalities, which may be made a means of annoyance, but which can never, I venture to think, be a source of strength; for adding to the resources of the public treasury, and for extending the uniform application of our system of government to those whose best interests we sincerely believe will be promoted thereby."

(Signed) DALHOUSIE.